91417

D1517508

Harper & Row

Cambridge, Hagerstown, New York, Philadelphia, Washington
London, Mexico City, São Paulo, Singapore, Sydney

This book is lovingly dedicated to Gwen Bradley, Nedra Callard, and Helen Peterson, who have consistently led their community through their vision and wisdom in providing better options for children and families and who continue to nurture us through our own stages of exploration.

The developmental affirmations for children on pages 11 to 13 are adapted from Pamela Levin's therapeutic affirmations in *Becoming the Way We Are* and are used with the permission of the author.

Cover design: Terry Dugan
Illustrations: Jerry Smath

Library of Congress Cataloging-in-Publication Data

Help! for parents of children ages six to eighteen months.

    (The Suggestion circle series; vol. 2)
    Includes index.
    1. Infants—Care and hygiene—United States.
2. Child rearing—United States.   I. Clarke, Jean Illsley.
II. Parents for parents.   III. Series.
HQ774.H445 1986   649'.122   86-18384
ISBN: 0-86683-452-4

   87 88 89 90 OPM 10 9 8 7 6 5   4   3   2

Contents

CLUSTERS AND SUGGESTION CIRCLES

Not crawling yet A-1...Not ready to share
A-2...Poking and pushing playmates A-3...
Jealousy A-4...Reading to baby A-5...Avoid-
ing sex role stereotyping A-6...Selecting shoes
for toddlers A-7...Stuck in one place A-8...
Preparing for sitter or day care A-9

Getting baby on schedule B-1...Sleeping
through the night B-2...Falling asleep without
nursing B-3...Screaming at bedtime B-4...
Fighting naptime B-5...Always wanting to be
rocked to sleep B-6...Climbing out of crib B-7

Mom worn out from nursing C-1...Nursing
baby refusing bottle C-2...Weaning from bottle C-3...Biting while nursing C-4...Pinching
Mom while nursing C-5...Others' opinions
C-6...Refusing baby food C-7...Refusing
cereals C-8...Finger food C-9...Refusing
meats C-10

649.122
Hel
copy 1

Appreciations

The Suggestion Circles in this book originated primarily in Yakima, Washington, through the schools' "Backyard Center" parent support groups. Additional Circles were offered by the following Yakima groups: Early Childhood program staff, La Leche League members, Yakima Valley College Cooperative Preschool parents, Educational Service District 105 parents, and Yakima community members. We appreciate these and the many Circles that were sent to us from other places by leaders of "Self-Esteem: A Family Affair" parenting classes.

Special plaudits are in order for the Yakima School District, a national leader in providing programs that support the belief that parents are the first and most vital teachers of their children.

Bounteous bouquets are sent to Laurie Kanyer, Carol Moore, Anne Rankin, Rosemary Rief, and Cathy Smart for their help with the project.

We thank Becky Monson and Mary Ann Lisk for their coordination skills, typing, and humor, pediatrician Christine Ternand, M.D., for editing the Circles for medical accuracy and for writing about abuse, and Deane Gradous for conceiving the idea of publishing Suggestion Circle Series.

And finally, hugs and kisses go to our families, who taught us that it is OK to try something new.

—The Editors

Foreword

Not very long ago, we were parenting four young ones— three adopted and one biological child. As each moved through the six- to eighteen-month stage of development, we had our share of concerns and always wished that we had a quick, ready resource to turn to in time of crisis. Having a creeper or toddler around the house meant that we were short on energy and time; we simply had no moments to thumb through pages and pages of the latest text on parenting. Oh, what we wouldn't have done for quick, creative suggestions from other parents!

With the variety of suggestions in this book, parents should be more able to support the exploration and experimentation of their six- to eighteen-month child and make more time for nurturing each other.

—Cy and Rosemary Rief
Originators of Yakima's first Backyard Center

What Is This Book About?

This is a book written for parents by parents.

It is for the days when you don't know what to do or when what you're doing isn't working. It is *not* a theoretical book about the times when things are going smoothly. It *is* a book of specific, practical suggestions for handling different problems that parents have sought help for in parenting classes around the country.

These parents have participated in groups led by a facilitator who is trained in the techniques used in the class, "Self-Esteem: A Family Affair." One of these techniques, called the "Suggestion Circle," is used to collect options for parents with problems. Here's how it works. In class, members sit in a circle and listen to a parent describe a problem. Each member of the Circle then offers his or her best suggestion for dealing with it. In this way, the person with the problem benefits from the collective wisdom and experience of the whole group and goes home with a list of suggestions or options.

The Suggestion Circle process is different from brainstorming, which encourages people to offer every idea that comes to mind. It's also different from listening to a teacher or an expert provide "the correct answer." In a Suggestion Circle, *every* answer comes from an "authority," that is, a parent, day-care provider, uncle, aunt, or grandparent. And every answer is "correct," since it worked for the person who discovered it—sometimes after many years of experience. The resulting list provides a variety of suggestions and encourages flexibility in the listener or reader. It may suggest a new way of perceiving the problem.

We chose these eighty-seven Circles because they represent problems that we hear about repeatedly in classes or that seem particularly difficult for parents. Leaders collected the suggestions and asked the parents if we could share their responses with you in these books. Each Circle includes the name of the first facilitator who sent the problem to us and the location of the class or group. Since similar problems come up in different parts of the country, we have combined suggestions from more than one group.

You will notice that often the answers contradict one another. That needn't bother you. Parents and children and homes are different and what works with one may not work with another or at another time. Use what works for you!

You will find the Suggestion Circles grouped in clusters according to subject matter. We have eliminated any ideas that advocated violence, both because child abuse is illegal and because we do not believe violence helps children. We have also eliminated suggestions that implied that parents or children are helpless or that a problem was not serious. We assume that if parents ask for help, the problems are important and serious to them.

In the opening pages of the book, we have outlined the *characteristic tasks of this stage* of development and described how parents may *abuse* children if they misunderstand those tasks. We have also given short explanations of *affirmations*, *recycling*, and other topics that are important parts of the "Self-Esteem: A Family Affair" class and that are referred to in the Circles.

So here they are, some short reference pieces and eighty-seven Circles, eighty-seven collections of the best ideas from parents who have been there, to you who are there now.

—The Editors

How to Use This Book

You can use this book to help you think. When you want ideas about how to solve a problem, look in the table of contents for a cluster title that seems to include your problem. For example, for a sleeping problem, look under "Now I Lay Me Down to Sleep." Or look in the index for words that describe your problem (like *sleep*, *bedtime*, or *nap*) and read about the problems that sound most like yours.

Reading about what other parents have done will remind you that there are many ways to solve problems and that you can discover and try out new ways that work for you and your child. If you read a list over several times, you will probably find ideas you missed the first time. Some of the suggestions may not fit your situation or your parenting style. Many of the lists contain contradictions, since there are lots of ways to raise children. Think about which suggestions sound useful for your particular problem.

Whenever you think of a suggestion that is not listed, write it in your book for future reference. *Our purpose is not to give "one right answer" but to support and stimulate your thinking by offering the wisdom of hundreds of the real child-rearing experts— parents themselves.*

Remember that these suggestions are *not* listed in an order of importance. They were offered by a circle of people. If we had printed them in circles, this would be a very big book! We offer them in lists to make a small and convenient book, not to imply that the top suggestion is best.

Use the short sections at the beginning and end of the book as you need them. For a picture of normal behavior, read **Ages and Stages** and **About Abuse**. You can use that information to think about whether your expectations are reasonable.

Affirmations for Growth is about healthy messages or beliefs that children this age need to decide are true for them. Ponder these affirming messages and all the ways, verbal and nonverbal, in which you offer these ideas regularly to your children. **Parents Get Another Chance— Recycling** reminds us that our own growth never stops and that we, too, are doing our developmental tasks.

Look at **How to Set Up a Child-Care Co-op,** or **How to Start a Backyard Center,** or **Where to Go for Additional Support**. If you want to lead your own **Suggestion Circle,** see page 122.

So read and think. Honor yourself for the many things you do well with your children. Celebrate your growth and the growth of your children. Change when you need to. Your parents did the best they could. You have been doing the best you can. If you want to learn some new ways of parenting, it is never too late to start.

Note: Throughout, we have alternated masculine and feminine pronouns; in one section or Circle, the child will be a "she," in the next a "he." Please read "all children."

—Jean Illsley Clarke

Ages and Stages

Here's what we know about six- to twelve-month-olds:

- They depend on adults to provide a safe and stimulating environment.
- They don't like to share their mother's time or attention with anyone.
- They want to be physically close to their mothers and may panic when she's out of sight.
- They can sit up and crawl.
- Some will walk. Many will not.
- They use their mouths a lot to check out things.
- They can grasp a cup or bottle with both hands and can manage finger foods.
- They can imitate simple actions like clapping hands and playing peek-a-boo.
- They begin to imitate new sounds.
- They like books that are sturdy and slobber proof with simple pictures.
- They may sleep anywhere from nine to eighteen hours a day.
- They may resist being put to bed around nine months.
- They are quite competent and can figure out solutions to many of their problems.

It is during the six- to twelve-month stage when "babies" turn into walking or near-walking one-year-olds. They have learned amazing skills and have grown tremendously. Let's go on to the twelve- to eighteen-month-old stage to see how these skills are refined and what new developments unfold.

Here's what we know about twelve- to eighteen-month-olds:
- They are constantly on the move.
- They can express whole thoughts with one word. ("Car" means "I want to go for a ride.")
- They can understand far more than they can express.
- They learn by doing.
- They cannot anticipate consequences or decide what's right or wrong.
- They may begin to resist naps.
- They like to play *alongside* other children.
- They like to stack blocks, pull things, fill and empty containers.
- They are *not* ready to be toilet-trained.
- They often intensely dislike having their hair washed.

  Exploration is the key word in describing this time in children's development. They are actually "soaking up" knowledge from everything they hear, touch, smell, and taste. So even if there are days when you imagine your child is "hyperactive," he is probably just a normal, curious, searching, and enthusiastic explorer!

—Darlene Montz, Judith L. Popp, and Judith-Anne Salts

About Abuse

Child abuse and neglect are prevalent and, perhaps, epidemic in our society today. We feel strongly that all children are to be valued and cherished. We believe that children will be better protected when parents know the causes and signs of child abuse and when they learn ways to keep children safe.

Causes of Child Abuse

There are many causes of child abuse. Since this is not a book about the ills of society or emotionally disturbed individuals but about normal, healthy parents and children, we will address only the abuse that springs from parents' misunderstanding of normal growth and development of children at different ages. Sometimes, as children go about their developmental tasks, they do things that are misinterpreted by parents who may be overly severe or hurtful in an attempt to stop or control those normal behaviors. Parents may believe that they are "disciplining," but when they punish their children for doing what is developmentally correct and normal, children are hurt physically or emotionally.

The following behaviors of children this age are frequently misunderstood:
- The toddler should be learning to explore and to trust his or her environment. Adults who misinterpret this activity as "getting into my things"

or "deliberately breaking things" or "messing up the place" may become inappropriately angry or even violent. Parents of toddlers can learn to cope by saying "Messy is beautiful" when their children are in this stage.

- Children at this age are active and curious, and supervising them is physically tiring to an adult. Tired adults are more likely to act and speak abusively in spite of their best intentions. Parents can cope by getting enough sleep and rest.
- Children this age are beginning to want some time and space away from others to develop their separateness. Caring adults sometimes respond by feeling rejected and then may reject the child emotionally. Parents can remember to refrain from interrupting the child whenever possible.

Signs of Child Abuse

Since other adults or older children may abuse toddlers, here are some physical signs that may indicate abuse of a child this age:

- Pin-size red marks around the eyes or blood in the white part of the eye may indicate that the child has been shaken.
- Circular bite marks, either adult- or child-size.
- Small, round burns from cigarettes.
- Hand slap marks on face or elsewhere.
- Bruised or tender fingertips from little hands being slapped.
- Bruises on the thighs or upper arms.
- Straight-line marks on the skin from abuse with a belt or a ruler.

Explorers need especially careful supervision for safety. Parents who do not abuse or neglect their children keep them safe by doing the following:

- Child-proofing their homes. One effective way to evaluate the safety in every room the child can enter is to lie on your stomach and see the exciting environment on the child's level. Remove or secure all dangerous attractions, especially cords and outlets, household chemicals, soaps, and medications.
- Carefully supervising a child in a walker, especially where there are open staircases. This is one of the biggest causes of toddler accidents.
- Carefully supervising play with older children, who sometimes hit or bite a younger sibling who is exploring their favorite possessions.
- Removing fragile, breakable objects from the explorer's environment for these few months.
- Refusing to leave a child alone in a house or car.
- Always using a car seat when traveling with a child in a car.
- Making certain that other adults who care for the child know how to support the child's need to explore. Ask them to think from a child's point of view and to figure out ways to protect the child without hitting or using harsh words.

If you suspect abuse of any kind, find a way to protect your child. Get help if you need it. Report the abuser to the child protection service in your area. See **Where to Go for Additional Help**.

—Christine Ternand, M.D.

Affirmations for Growth

At each period or stage of growth in children's lives there are certain tasks they need to master and certain decisions they need to make if they are to grow into loving, capable, responsible adults.

Parents can help children master these tasks by providing safe, structured, stimulating environments and experiences. Parents can encourage their children to make appropriate decisions by giving their children affirmations.

What are affirmations? Affirmations are all the things we do or say that imply that children are lovable and capable. We affirm children with our words and our actions, our body language, our facial expression, and our tone of voice.

Here are some special affirming messages that will help children during this stage of growth. At this stage they explore their environment and learn to trust their senses. They must leave the lap and the crib and explore their world in order to develop their intelligence, their sense of self, and their ability to do things.

Affirmations for Doing

- You can explore and experiment, and I will support and protect you.
- You can use all of your senses when you explore.
- You can do things as many times as you need to.
- You can know what you know.

- You can be interested in everything.
- I like to watch you initiate and grow and learn.
- I love you when you are active and when you are quiet.

You *give* these affirming messages by the way you interact with your child and by providing a safe environment in which the child can move freely about. You can also *say* or sing the affirmations. Children seem to understand, perhaps from your tone of voice and your caring actions, what they mean.

Of course, you have to believe the affirmations yourself, or they come off as confusing or conflicting messages. In order for your child to believe them, it must be truly important to you that your child try things, initiate things, explore things, and be curious and intuitive. Also, you must be happy with your child because she is unique and not just respond joyfully to the little tricks that children learn. If children believe that they don't have to be cute or clever or sad or mad or scared or amusing or smart or delicate or macho or fragile for you to love them, they are encouraged to grow. They can learn to trust their senses, to believe in their own ability to learn and to understand the environment and themselves.

Since we never outgrow the need for these health-giving messages, children at this age continue to need the Being affirmations from the infant stage, which are about the right to exist and have needs.

Affirmations for Being

- I'm glad you are alive.
- You belong here.
- What you need is important.
- I'm glad you are you.
- You can grow at your own pace.
- You can feel all of your feelings.
- I love you, and I care for you willingly.

Being messages are important for people of all ages. Children who didn't decide to believe all these messages as infants have another chance to incorporate them now. Remember, it is never too late for you to start giving these affirmations.

You can read more about what affirmations mean and don't mean and how to use them in families in Clarke's *Self-Esteem: A Family Affair*. These affirmations are adapted from Pamela Levin's *Becoming the Way We Are*. (See **Resources**.)

When you discover additional affirmations that your child needs, write them in your book and give them to your child.

—Jean Illsley Clarke

Parents Get Another Chance—
Recycling

Parents of toddlers have an important, sometimes exhausting job caring for their busy explorers. One of the benefits for parents of this period of children's growth is that the parents get a chance to experience their worlds anew through the eyes and antics of their child and to recycle their own need to see things in new and exciting ways.

What Is Recycling?

Recycling is the name given to the rhythmic, cyclical growth process that individuals go through, often without noticing it, in which they learn to do important developmental tasks in ever more competent and sophisticated ways. The theory is described in Pamela Levin's *Becoming the Way We Are*. Recycling does not mean that we adults regress to a childlike state, but rather that our life experiences demand that we continually develop more skillful ways of doing life supporting tasks. Besides having a natural rhythm of our own, we parents often recycle or upgrade the tasks of the stages our children are in. I have talked with hundreds of parents about this idea. Many of them have reported, often with some surprise, that they *are* working on some of the same tasks as their children. It is a normal, healthy, and hopeful aspect of living with growing children.

Parents, especially if they have been at home full-time with an infant, often experience renewed energy and a heightened interest in "doing something" around the time the child reaches six or seven months. Because of this urge to reach out for different experiences and activities, the parent often seems more alert and suddenly restless.

Parents can use this energy to find new things to explore. They may renew activities that they had dropped during their child's infancy. Sometimes they take up a new hobby or sport, or take some time away from that busy toddler for lessons they have been promising themselves for years. By doing this, parents increase their own ability to explore the adult world.

The affirmations that are helpful to our children are also healthy for us. (See page 11.) Because many of us decided not to believe some of those healthy messages or only to believe them partly, this is an ideal time to accept those messages for ourselves and to claim more of our ability to be whole, healthy, joyful adults. If you didn't get the affirmations you needed first time around, you can take them now as you offer them to your children.

—Jean Illsley Clarke

A. The Nature of the Toddler

My seven-month-old does not crawl yet. I'm worried.

- Don't worry! Children develop at their own rate.
- Provide lots of chances for the baby to be on her tummy on the floor.
- To ease your worry, ask your physician or public health nurse to see if your child's development is normal. Most children at this age don't crawl, but they do act alert and roll over.
- Read a book about developmental stages: for example, Brazelton's *Infants and Mothers* or Leach's *Your Baby & Child*. (See **Resources**.)
- Don't be in a hurry to advance your child to a new stage of development.
- Be sure her clothes are loose and comfortable; and allow her to be naked for short periods.
- Don't get hooked by what relatives or friends say *their* children did.
- Put something interesting or entrancing just out of reach when she is on her tummy.
- Relax and enjoy. She will take off soon enough.

(See also H-10.)

Thanks to Backyard Center Parents, Circle from Yakima, Washington

How can I feel better about my child's not being ready to share? He is fourteen months old.

- A fourteen-month-old may hand things to another child, but sharing is a very mature concept. Lots of adults don't do it well.
- Play games that encourage him to pass things back and forth.
- My children didn't share well until after kindergarten.
- Have enough toys and pots and pans for all the toddlers.
- Avoid taking the child to places where he needs to share.
- Children this age play *near* each other, not *with* each other. Read *Baby Learning Through Baby Play* by Gordon. (See **Resources**.)
- Don't expect him to share a favorite toy yet. He's too young.
- Help him get ready for sharing by passing the cookies when there are enough for everyone.
- Remember, at his age it is like asking you to open your bank account to a friend. You probably wouldn't like that.

(See also D-3.)

Thanks to Backyard Center Parents, Circle from Yakima, Washington

What should I do when my thirteen-month-old pokes, pushes, and pulls on playmates?

- Say, "That hurts. If you want to pull on something, you can pull on this," and offer something acceptable like a rag doll.
- Touch both children and talk to them calmly. The book *Infancy and Caregiving* by Gonzalez-Mena and Eyer tells how to do this. (See **Resources**.)
- Say, "Here are two things you can poke."
- A favorite game for this age is Investigating Faces— especially poking at eyes and mouth. Guide her hand as she touches your eyes and say, "Gently, gently." Refer to Segal's book, *From One to Two Years*. (See **Resources**.)
- Don't interfere unless the other child is upset or in danger of being injured.

(See also D-1, D-4, G-8.)

Thanks to Backyard Center Parents, Circle from Yakima, Washington

My son gets upset when Mom or Grandma holds another child or directs her attention elsewhere. He throws himself down on the floor and cries.

- Give him a teddy bear to hold while you hold the other child.
- Act bored with his tantrum.
- Remember that it is normal at his age not to want to share his mom.
- At another time rock your son and say, "There is enough holding for you."
- Make sure Mom or Grandma has special time with him later that day.
- Have Grandma continue to hold the other child while you move closer to your son. Just be there by him.
- Before the problem arises, encourage your son to join in singing a song to the child being held, perhaps a funny song.
- Don't make fun of your son or shame him.
- Get a rocking chair that is big enough to hold both of them at once.
- Say, "When you want to be held, I expect you to ask."

(See also E-7.)

Thanks to Backyard Center Parents, Circle from Yakima, Washington

When should I start reading to my baby, and what should I read? She doesn't pay attention to anything for very long.

- Look at a simple picture book together each day.
- Pick books that have one large picture per page, pictures that are good for naming and pointing to objects.
- Include the baby when you're reading to your older child.
- Read a few sentences out loud from whatever you are reading: recipes, newspapers, or magazine articles.
- Allow your child to play with and even mangle some adult books.
- You can expect a very short attention span at this age. She may stay interested for two minutes or less.
- Provide cloth books your child can chew on and crumple.
- Make storytime a special time for physical closeness with your baby, cuddling her when she allows it.
- Repeat favorite nursery rhymes throughout the day while bathing, diapering, or riding in the car. Occasionally show her nursery rhyme books.
- Use very stiff board books. The baby may rather open and close the book than be read to.
- Give her old magazines to look at and tear up.
- Start today.

Thanks to Backyard Center Parents, Circle from Yakima, Washington

There is so much talk lately about sex-role stereotyping. How can I avoid stereotyping with my fifteen-month-old son?

- Teach your child to feel good about his own gender. Say, "I'm glad you are a boy," and "I surely do love you, son."
- When both spouses work around the house, doing all kinds of chores and taking care of children, your son will see that both men and women do many things.
- Offer him a variety of toys such as blocks, pull toys, and dolls.
- Take him to a woman doctor.
- Don't limit the father-son interaction to roughhousing.
- Don't be afraid of your boy child playing house with dolls. He needs practice in nurturing skills.
- Follow your child's interests. Let him do what he wants, regardless of sex.
- Be sure to hug, love, and cuddle both little boys and little girls, and let your son see you do it.
- Give your son lots of hugging and touching.
- Take a look at the decor of his bedroom: Does it suggest that he should play football or hunt? Or is it a colorful room that reflects children at play?
- Don't handle him more roughly than you would a girl, and don't tell him that boys don't cry.

(See also H-11, I-4.)

Thanks to Backyard Center Parents, Circle from Yakima, Washington

My baby will be walking soon. What should I know about selecting shoes for her?

- Choose tennis shoes or shoes with soft soles for warmth and safety out-of-doors.
- Bare feet and booties are OK for indoors.
- Take her with you when you are buying shoes to see that she gets a good fit.
- Select shoes with treads. They're safer.
- Feel the inside of the shoe to be sure it doesn't have rough edges.
- Many learning-to-walk babies like to go barefoot. They have better balance.
- Look for shoes with a good, firm arch.
- Get straps or laces to keep the shoes on.
- It's OK to use shoes another child has used if the shoes are worn evenly and fit properly.

Thanks to Backyard Center Parents, Circle from Yakima, Washington

What are some things I can do when I'm "stuck in one place" with my explorer?

- Bring several plastic eggs or small paper bags filled with favorite toys and/or various snacks like raisins, Cheerios, or fish crackers.
- Bring along a favorite book of nursery rhymes.
- Play peek-a-boo and patty-cake, sing songs and do finger plays, or name and touch parts of the child's body.
- Keep a pencil and a pad of paper in your purse.
- Bring along a straw to blow "soft breezes" on arms, legs, and tummy.
- Fill a special sack or purse with toys used only for "going out" times. Consider including a soft ball.
- Before heading out, visualize yourself as having lots of patience. Be in the right mood!
- Find a "feely" book for your child to touch, like *Pat the Bunny* by Dorothy Kunhardt. (See **Resources**.)
- Toys that stack work well and take little space.
- When you can, choose a family-oriented place "to be stuck in."

(See also E-5, F-1.)

Thanks to Yakima Valley Community College, Circle from Cooperative Preschool Parents, Yakima, Washington

How can I prepare my child for being in a babysitter's care or at day care?

- Practice separation at home in the early months. Tell your child when you are going into another room and then come back quickly.
- Play games like Peek-A-Boo and Guess Which Hand to assure your child that things do exist even though she can't see them.
- Being afraid of strangers is normal at this stage, so exchange sitting with friends for a while rather than leave your daughter with strangers.
- Tell your child where you are going and who will be with her.
- Tell the sitter about any special fears or preferences your explorer has and the best ways to comfort her when she cries.
- Before you go away for the first time, have the babysitter come several times to stay for a few minutes while you are there. Pay the sitter for these visits.
- Establish a ritual at home for getting ready (packing favorite toys or blanket).
- Stay with the child the first time. Then leave for short periods, gradually increasing the time you are away.
- Prepare a special snack for your child to eat while she is with the sitter.

(See also I-3, I-8.)

Thanks to Backyard Center Parents, Circle from Yakima, Washington

B. Now I Lay Me Down to Sleep

How can I get my baby on a schedule?

- Try keeping the same *sequence* of activities instead of worrying about a specific time schedule.
- Follow your child's own natural "schedule." Set a schedule that is based on her rhythms.
- Play the same soothing lullaby each time you put her to bed.
- See if establishing a bedtime ritual, such as a warm bath or warm bottle, will "cue" your baby that it is bedtime.
- When your baby begins to eat solids and finger foods, aim for regular mealtimes.
- Be aware that some babies go on schedules more easily than others.
- When you realize that the schedule is for your own convenience rather than for the baby, you will see that you need to find time for yourself *and* fit into the baby's rhythms.
- If you sometimes change the baby's bedtime to suit you, don't expect her to go back on schedule automatically.

(See also B-3, H-3.)

Thanks to Yakima Valley College, Circle from Cooperative Preschool Parents, Yakima, Washington

My thirteen-month-old wakes up two or three times during the night. What can I do?

- Be patient. It may just be his age. New walkers sometimes move their legs as though walking during light sleep. He may be waking himself up with all this activity.
- He could be teething and having more pain and pressure in his mouth when he is prone. Try a pillow.
- Take him to bed with you.
- Listen to the sleep tape, *Infant and Toddler Sleep Disruptions*, by Saul L. Brown, M.D. (See **Resources**.)
- Leave a humidifier or radio on softly for "white" noise.
- Go in, lay him down, pat his back, tell him you love him, and then leave. Don't go back into his room until he wakes the next time.
- Leave him at home with grandparents for a night. Check into a motel and get some sleep.
- Nap during the day when he naps. (Take the phone off the hook.)
- Try feeding him solids before bedtime.
- Try a pacifier. Don't play with him.
- Keep him awake during the morning and early evening so he doesn't sleep more than five hours during the day.
- Avoid rigorous play just before bedtime.

(See also H-4, H-5.)

Thanks to Ellen Peterson, Circle from Orinda, California

How can I get my baby to go to sleep without nursing her?

- Very calmly give her a warm bath just before bed.
- Offer her a pacifier.
- Rock your daughter in her room and sing to her.
- Put on a record of the same soothing music every night just before bedtime.
- Give her a drink of milk from a cup just before bed.
- If *you* want to continue nursing at bedtime, why not?
- See that she has a bottle of water.
- Establish a nice bedtime ritual, with lots of cuddling and soothing talk.
- Mom can be part of the early ritual, but someone else can put the baby into bed.
- Don't get discouraged. Your daughter has been nursing all her life. It may take days or even weeks for her to get used to the new routine.

(See also B-1, C-1, C-2.)

Thanks to Backyard Center Parents, Circle from Yakima, Washington

My sixteen-month-old screams so hard at bedtime
he has a bowel movement. If he falls asleep on the
couch he wakes up and screams when moved. My
doctor and my sister are warning me to let him cry
it out. I feel terrible about that.

- Hum with him. Walk, sway, and use a low voice.
  Calm him down.
- Turn off the light. Hold him, sway and rock.
- Establish a routine as to who carries him in to
  bed, saying good night to everyone. Talk quietly
  to him.
- Don't blame yourself.
- If his stools are hard or blood streaked, tell your
  physician.
- When you are sure he is cared for, let him cry for
  ten minutes for three nights. See if that works.
- Place the mattress on the floor instead of in the
  crib.
- Remember that your physician is a *medical*
  specialist and doesn't have to listen to your
  child's screams. Trust your own feelings.
- Stay in your son's room. Talk quietly to him so
  he knows you are there.
- Ask your physician to examine your child to be
  sure he doesn't have something wrong with his
  bowels.

(See also B-1, B-3, B-5, E-7, G-4.)

Thanks to Ellen Peterson, Circle from Orinda,
California

Our seventeen-month-old used to be a good "napper." Now all of a sudden she cries and fusses, and fights taking a nap.

- Take her for a walk in the fresh air just before she takes a nap.
- Try adjusting naptime to an hour later than usual and shorten it.
- Lie down with your baby. You deserve some rest, too.
- Establish a routine. Say the same "time to nap" words or play a lullaby record as you put her to bed.
- Make the room dark and quiet. Turn the lights and TV off. Pull the shades down.
- Read a story to cue the child to quiet down. If she doesn't seem to fall asleep after that, let her quietly look at some stiff-board books in her crib.
- Sing quietly to the baby for several minutes. Then leave the room.
- Rock her for a while before naptime.
- Gently massage her before you lay her down.
- Babies need less sleep as they grow older. Maybe she is ready to skip naps.

(See also B-4, B-7.)

Thanks to Sue Hansen, Circle from Bellevue, Washington

How can I get my son to go into his crib while he is still awake? I always end up rocking him to sleep.

- Decide on a certain amount of time to rock him (five to ten minutes) and then put him to bed. Decrease the time a little each night.
- Just make up your mind that you'll put him to bed while he's still awake and follow through. Babies can sense if you are unsure about your decision.
- Use a flannel sheet for warmth or give him a special blanket or toy he can become attached to and use for comfort.
- Allow at least three nights of crying before you expect a change.
- Get a cradle that rocks automatically and let it rock him to sleep.
- Tape the noise of a vacuum cleaner and play the tape before going to bed. Or use soft music or a clock.
- Remember that some babies do not need as much sleep as others and will have a more difficult time dozing off.
- Stuff your most used piece of clothing, like a T-shirt or nightgown, into the baby's crib so he will be reassured by your scent.
- Read *Crying Baby, Sleepless Nights* by Sandy Jones. (See **Resources**.)

(See B-5, B-7.)

Thanks to Backyard Center Parents, Circle from Yakima, Washington

How do you handle a child who has just learned to climb out of her crib?

- Stand outside her door. When she begins to crawl out, say firmly, "Go back to bed."
- If she can't get down safely, figure out a way to keep her safe so she doesn't fall on her head.
- Put her back in bed *every time* she climbs out.
- Lay the mattress on the floor.
- Tell her, "I like the way you stay in bed" every time she is staying there.
- Try a youth bed.
- See if there is a lower adjustment level for the mattress and drop the mattress down a few inches.
- Switch to a twin-size bed with a portable side railing.

Thanks to Nancy Bergerson, Circle from Minnetonka, Minnesota

C. Nursing, Feeding, and Weaning

My baby is six months old. I want to continue nursing, but I'm all worn out.

- The important emotional nurturing you are providing is an investment in your baby's future. Try to nap or go to bed early, at least every other day.
- Check your diet. Often strains or impatience come from lack of energy.
- See your doctor and ask for help with feeling better.
- Try not to do so much. Don't take on additional responsibilities.
- Go for walks; sunshine increases vitamin D. It helps your skin and your outlook.
- Call another nursing mom and compare ideas.
- Decide if you want to continue and then be OK with your decision.
- Nursing allows a portable baby.
- Pamper yourself. Go out to dinner.
- Trade off babysitting to get some time just for yourself.

(See also H-4, H-5.)

Thanks to La Leche League, Circle from Yakima, Washington

I'm trying to get my seven-month-old baby to take a bottle instead of nursing all the time. He doesn't want anything to do with the bottle. Do you have any ideas?

- Use a nipple shield on your breast to get him used to the feel of the nipple.
- See if using different formulas will help.
- Give him time to get used to the bottle. It is a big change for both of you.
- Try different nipples for bottles and adjust the size of the holes.
- Pump your breast. Offer only the expressed milk in the bottle for a while.
- Ask your husband to give your son the bottle. You may want to leave the room or even leave the house.
- That's a big transition for your little one and for you, too. Neither one of you has to hurry!
- He may adjust better to a cup than to a bottle.
- Your baby might like some of the new bottles on the market, especially the ones with the Disney characters.
- See what the hospital nursery staff or your doctor can offer for suggestions.

(See also B-3, C-3.)

Thanks to Backyard Center Parents, Circle from Yakima, Washington

My explorer is fifteen months old and she still wants her bottle. How can I get her off the bottle?

• Put your child's favorite drinks in a cup.
• Find her a fun cup that has pictures on the bottom or maybe a built-in straw.
• Offer your explorer beverages in her cup several times a day, when you take a coffee break.
• Don't rush. Let the child choose the right time.
• Put water only in the bottle.
• Make a placemat with outline drawings of a plate, cup, and silverware. Your child's cup then will have its own special spot.
• Both of you have fun while you're feeding solids and using a cup! Babies sometimes miss the closeness and attention more than the bottle.
• Think about why you want her off the bottle. We all have oral needs. Some of us smoke or chew gum.
• Rock your child and sing to her instead of giving her a bottle.
• My physician explained that water in a bottle is OK as long as the baby wants it. Sugared fluids like milk and juice may cause cavities.

(See also C-2.)

Thanks to Backyard Center Parents, Circle from Yakima, Washington

My baby bites me when nursing. How can I get him to stop?

- When he bites, stop nursing immediately.
- Stick your finger into the baby's mouth to relieve the suction.
- Explain that it hurts. Say, "No, that hurts."
- If your child is teething, offer him something else to bite.
- Change your position. Maybe lie down.
- Try the football hold to change your baby's position: hold your baby close to your body with his head in your hand, his body on your forearm, and his feet between your upper arm and body.
- Pull down on his chin and say firmly, "Don't bite." Wait a few seconds and return to nursing.
- Decide if your child is really hungry. If he's not serious about nursing, don't let him dawdle.
- Watch his expression. Maybe you can anticipate the bite.

(See also E-4.)

Thanks to La Leche League, Circle from Yakima, Washington

My seven-month-old baby won't let go of me while she is nursing. She holds onto my arm so tight that she bruises it. What can I do?

- Hold her hand during nursing.
- Position your child so you can give her your finger to hold.
- See that she is in a comfortable position with secure support under her.
- Stroke her arm to help her relax and sing to her.
- Talk to her gently and look into her eyes. Make nursing a special time together.
- Don't let her bruise you. Take her hand gently away and give her a soft toy to hold.
- Try a pad of some kind under your arm so she can't get hold of your skin.
- Get in a different position for nursing. Try lying down with her beside you, keeping her head slightly elevated.

Thanks to Nat Houtz, Circle from Seattle, Washington

I've been nursing my baby for seven months, and I'm constantly questioned as to when I'm going to stop. The question I'm asked is, "Are you *still* nursing?"

- Give them a date. Say, "I plan to nurse at least ten months."
- Say, "Yes, isn't it wonderful? My doctor is so proud of me!"
- Join a nursing mothers' support group. They have terrific answers to questions like this.
- State that closeness is good for babies, and this is one way to give it.
- Say "yes" in a factual, nonemotional, I-have-no-more-to-say tone.
- This gives you the chance to teach them all about immunity, closeness, touching, and babies' need to suck.
- Tell them to read *Touching* by Ashley Montagu. It tells why babies need lots of touch. (See **Resources**.)
- Stress that nursing is a personal relationship between you and your child and that it helps the baby bond with you.
- Tell them he will only be a baby once, and if he is going to get nursing he has to get it now.
- Say, "Yes, this is one thing his father can't do."
- Say, "Why do you ask?" and then decide whether you want to respond or not.

(See also G-4, I-6.)

Thanks to La Leche League, Circle from Yakima, Washington

I can't get my seven-month-old baby to eat baby food. Should I be concerned?

- Concerned, yes, tense, no. Children go on food spurts. Don't worry.
- Feed her what she likes. Don't be concerned about preferences at this age.
- Don't force her to eat.
- Try introducing small amounts of food at different times during the day.
- Notice your child's best-mood time and try some baby food then.
- Watch for allergies. Try only one food for a few days at a time until you find one she likes.
- Ask your doctor if vitamins are needed to supplement her diet.
- Try making your own baby food rather than buying the commercial brands. Just put your unsalted table foods into a blender.
- If you are nursing, don't worry about it yet. Breast milk is a good diet for your baby if you are eating well.
- Let your child put her hands in the food so she can lick her fingers.
- If your child isn't underweight, don't make a mountain out of a spoonful of beans.

(See also C-8.)

Thanks to Backyard Center Parents, Circle from Yakima, Washington

My baby has been eating solids for quite a few months, and now he won't eat baby cereals.

- Trust him. Perhaps he has a slight allergy to cereal.
- Try a different type of cereal.
- Omit cereal for a while and try again later.
- Put finger treats on his tray, like puffed wheat or Cheerios.
- Give your child the grains he needs in other ways — like muffins or cornbread.
- See if he would like some old-fashioned cream of wheat or oatmeal instead of "pasty" baby cereal. Perhaps baby cereal is boring to him now.
- Make edible play dough out of whole wheat flour, water, and instant rice, and let him play with it.
- Don't wheedle, scold, or force.

(See also C-7.)

Thanks to Backyard Center Parents, Circle from Yakima, Washington

My baby is starting to eat finger food and I'm concerned about protein intake for my baby.

- Try frozen chicken or fish sticks cut up into finger-size pieces.
- Do you know that a one-inch cube of cheese equals one-half cup of milk?
- You might get a small tabletop grinder and grind table foods for the baby right at the table. She'll love to watch it being ground and may be more interested in trying it.
- In *Your Baby & Child*, Penelope Leach says that an average size ten-month-old needs about twenty grams of protein. So if she takes one pint of milk, that takes care of sixteen grams already. (See **Resources**.)
- My kids love yogurt, especially yogurt pops and cottage cheese with fruit mixed in.
- Try grilled cheese sandwich strips, French toast squares, quiche cubes, and peanut butter toast.
- Offer your child a variety of food from all four food groups and then relax. My doctor says the typical American diet contains too much protein.
- Babies know how much they need to eat. Just make sure that what you give her is nutritious and not junk food.
- Put some soybean in her food. Soybean protein is almost a perfect substitute for animal protein.

(See also C-10.)

Thanks to Backyard Center Parents, Circle from Yakima, Washington

I want my fouteen-month-old baby to eat ground meats or baby meats, but he just spits them out. I'm worried about him getting a balanced diet. What do you recommend?

- Try baby-food chicken or beef sticks. They look like Vienna sausages but are not spicy.
- Make spaghetti with hamburger or baby meats in it.
- Avoid red meats for a few months. Offer chicken or turkey.
- Mix the meat with rice, bread, or anything he does like.
- Look for substitute foods that have similar mineral and vitamin content such as cheese, fish, or lentil soup.
- This is probably a phase that will pass. Perhaps he doesn't like the texture.
- Buy wafer thin, sliced meat and cut it into small pieces.
- Try cheese or cottage cheese.
- Let him see you grind your own meat in a blender or in a small hand grinder, especially for him.
- If your baby is getting a balanced diet, you could avoid meats for a while.
- Don't talk with your child about it. He is not a bad person for not wanting meats.

(See also C-9.)

Thanks to Backyard Center Parents, Circle from Yakima, Washington

D. Siblings and Such

How can I keep my explorer out of my older girl's toys?

- Tell your daughter to keep her special toys in her own room. Keep the baby out.
- Use an actual physical barrier (gate or "fencing off") to keep the children separate for short periods.
- Ask your daughter which toys she wants to share, and keep those in the family room. "Separate" toys can be kept in other places.
- Tell your girl to put away her special toys when she is done playing with them.
- Let your daughter know it is OK to have "private" toys.
- Get your older child a little chest with a combination lock.
- Let your daughter use the playpen as a hideaway where she can play without being disturbed.
- Give the explorer a basket of his own toys to divert his attention.
- Have special time with the young one during the time your daughter is playing with personal toys or projects.
- Put the baby in a high chair with Cheerios or other finger foods sometimes.

(See also A-3, D-3, F-2.)

Thanks to Ellen Peterson, Circle from Walnut Creek, California

How can I give my second child as much attention and as many opportunities as I did my first child?

- Realistically, there just isn't as much time for the second child as there was for the first. I would just shoot for special time with the younger child—quality instead of quantity.
- Family activities with your explorer can make up for lots of things you did individually with the first child.
- Look into starting a neighborhood playgroup for your older child. When the group is at another family's home, use this time to do special things with your explorer.
- Constantly trying to keep everything "even-steven" makes for very competitive kids. Also it can be wearing. Your needs are important, too, so take care of your own spiritual and intellectual needs.
- Schedule naps at different times so both children have individual time with you.
- Ask your older child to do some special activities with your explorer for short periods of time.
- Hire an older youngster in the neighborhood to come over a couple of times a week to play with one of them while you spend time with the other.
- Look at the experiences your explorer is getting that your preschooler didn't get. Your second child is learning a lot from his big brother.

(See also D-5, I-2.)

Thanks to Marilyn Grevstad, Circle from Seattle, Washington

My three-year-old constantly grabs toys away from the baby—ones that aren't even his. What can I do to stop this?

- Spend special time daily with the three-year-old without interruption.
- Watch. When the older child shows signs of sharing, praise him.
- Pay more positive attention to the three-year-old.
- Encourage the older child to tell you when he offers a toy to the baby and then praise him.
- Say, "I expect you to find things for you to do and to let the baby have his toys."
- Have certain toys just for the baby and let the three-year-old do some things that the baby can't do.
- Make some time when you keep the baby out of the three-year-old's projects.
- Catch the three-year-old being good. Praise him when he hasn't grabbed toys away from the baby.
- Buy some items for the baby only, and some for the three-year-old only.

(See also A-2, D-1, D-4.)

Thanks to Backyard Center Parents, Circle from Yakima, Washington

My two-and-a-half-year-old nephew takes toys away and hits my one-year-old son whenever we have family gatherings. I need suggestions on what to do so I can enjoy these outings without worrying about protecting my son.

- Decide when it is critical for safety reasons to intervene and when you can let the children work it out. Read *Infants and Mothers* or *Toddlers and Parents* by Brazelton. (See **Resources.**)
- Ask your brother and sister-in-law to split the time of watching the children with you.
- Consider leaving the baby at home with a sitter.
- Tell the older child he is not to hit the baby, and give him something else to hit instead.
- Give the older child a doll or teddy bear of his own to practice being gentle with.
- Do whatever you need to do to stop the hitting. Your baby does not need that.
- It is OK to protect the baby yourself. Keep your son out of your nephew's reach.
- Ask the boy's parents what they can do to stop the hitting.
- Your child needs protection. One way you can lessen your worry is to take a competent babysitter with you to protect your child.
- Tell his parents how you feel. Ask them to be in charge of their son's behavior.

(See also D-3, H-9.)

Thanks to Backyard Center Parents, Circle from Yakima, Washington

How can I get my three-year-old daughter to be more positively involved with the baby?

- Tell your older kids stories about them when they were tiny. This helps them realize how special they are.
- When you can, give extra special time to your daughter so she won't view the new baby as a threat. It's even fun to splash through a mud puddle together.
- Catch your daughter being good with the baby. Comment on her helpfulness and good behavior.
- Show your three-year-old how to behave and to gently handle and play with the younger child. You could buy a doll for her to practice with.
- Allow the older child to help you in taking care of the younger one.
- Watch what you say. She may not understand "Be nice." Saying, "Be gentle," or "Touch softly," while you demonstrate it, tells her what to do.
- Talk with your daughter about her feelings—that some days she may be jealous and not always "like" the baby and that her feelings are OK.
- While your three-year-old is within earshot, tell the baby how lucky he is to have such a helpful big sister.

(See also D-2.)

Thanks to Backyard Center Parents, Circle from Yakima, Washington

With only two bedrooms in our home, should the baby sleep in our room or in her brother's room?

- One solution is moving, but if you can't, don't put her in your bedroom. You need to sleep. Put the baby in the living room, and she won't bother your other child. When the baby starts to sleep for longer periods of time, put her in with her brother.

- It is difficult to remove your child from your bedroom once you start letting her sleep there. Your baby will sleep through more interruptions if exposed to household activities and noises.

- *The Family Bed* by Tine Thevenin has lots of suggestions. Having your baby in the room with you is convenient, and then you can nurse the baby in bed. (See **Resources**.)

- Look for a solution that fits your needs, the baby's needs, and your spouse's needs.

- If you take the baby to your room, use your intuition as to when to move the baby, so she doesn't stay in your room too long.

- If your baby is sleeping through the night most of the time, let her join her brother.

- Ask your three-year-old to help prepare a spot for the baby in his room.

- You may really like having your baby sleep next to your bed.

- Don't have intercourse while the baby is in the room.

Thanks to Mary Pannanen, Circle from Seattle, Washington

We're considering having another baby. What do you think about spacing kids?

• The ideal for me was to have one child out of diapers before I had another.

• Read Burton White's *The First Three Years of Life*. He says the ideal is to space children at least three years apart. (See **Resources**.)

• Four or five years is even better because the older child has his own world at school.

• There is no right or wrong. There are difficulties with any age spread.

• At three, the sibling is more independent and has less need of Mom's attention than earlier. The child understands more about Mom's having a baby and can express herself.

• I know of a family where the children are sixteen months apart. Right now it is very hard on both Mom and children.

• If you have your children close together to get it over with, you may not have enough time for each one.

• Space them at least two-and-a-half to three years apart.

• If you wait seven to ten years between children, it extends parenting for a long time and keeps you young longer.

• Perhaps consider only one. I was one and found it a positive experience, as there isn't any competition or jealousy.

Thanks to Backyard Center Parents, Circle from Yakima, Washington

E. Coping with the Explorer

How can I keep my son from turning into a wrestler every time I change his diapers?

- Use diversionary tactics. Try dangling toys from your mouth to catch his attention.
- Use some musical toys on the changing table. Switch to different toys or a different table for variety.
- Hold your child calmly for a few moments and tell him you love him before you start to change him.
- Save special toys to keep him occupied during diaper changing.
- Keep a firm grip and say calmly, "Lie still. Stay here." Make sure the firm grip is not abusive.
- The book *Infancy and Caregiving* by Gonzalez-Mena and Eyer tells how to talk to the baby, telling him what you are doing and getting his cooperation every step of the way. (See **Resources**.)
- Wind up a music box, and both of you can sing along while you change his diapers.
- Play the body parts game, "Show Me Your Ears," and teach him new parts during changing time.

Thanks to Backyard Center Parents, Circle from Yakima, Washington

My daughter is seventeen months old and I have a terrible battle washing her hair. Any suggestions?

- A few times wash her hair without soap and see if that helps.
- Make sure the water is not too hot or cold and don't rush her.
- Tell her favorite stories with lots of expression during the shampoo.
- To stop water from running into her eyes at shampoo time, lay her on the counter and place a folded washcloth on her forehead. Tell her to look up and ask her what she sees. Make it a game.
- Use washcloth shampoos for a while. She might be afraid of water splashing in her nose and mouth.
- Give her plenty of water playtime *before* the shampoo.
- Remember you are a good parent even when you don't wash her hair every single day!
- Use a shampoo that doesn't sting the eyes.
- Let her choose how she wants her hair washed— in the tub or lying on her back on the counter by the sink.
- My boys enjoyed hair washing lots more after I let them wash my hair first.

Thanks to Backyard Center Parents, Circle from Yakima, Washington

Give me some hints for cutting my son's fingernails without drawing blood.

• Cut them while he is asleep.

• Have Dad cut them while your son nurses.

• Cut them with blunt-end scissors that are especially made for babies.

• Trim your son's fingernails while he is on your lap. Talk to him, and hold his hand out in front of you.

• Do the task when he is at his best physically. Also make certain that you are not tired or in a hurry.

• Try an emery board instead of scissors.

• Have someone else keep your son busy looking at something while you trim. Sing while you cut.

• Play a game in which each finger has a special name.

Thanks to Backyard Center Parents, Circle from Yakima, Washington

My fourteen-month-old bites me when I am holding her. What can I do to stop her?

- Put your daughter down when she does it and pick her up later.
- Hold her away from you and say, "Ouch!" Let her know you hurt.
- Say, "Stop it!" in a very stern voice.
- Use a startling voice.
- Make eye contact with her and say firmly, "No biting!"
- Offer her something that is OK to bite on. Then demonstrate by putting a wooden spoon or a plastic toy in your mouth.
- Put safe things into her mouth.
- Tell her, "People are not for biting."
- Your child may be trying to imitate kissing and perhaps is confused about how to kiss. Show her how to purse her lips.
- She may be teething. Massage her jaw or give her a rubber toy, a bagel, or a frozen banana to chew on.
- Snap a teething ring on a short ribbon to the shoulder of her sleeper.

(See also C-4, E-10.)

Thanks to Nancy Drake and Ellen Peterson, Circle from Walnut Creek, California

We're going on a long car trip. What can we do to entertain our sixteen-month-old?

• Take finger foods and drinks that are easy to eat.
• Leave during the night or at regular naptime.
• Make a cassette tape of songs and rhymes to play during travel.
• Keep formula prepared in a thermos or stop to nurse him when needed.
• Stop every hour and let the baby crawl or run.
• Take things to keep the child busy—books, games, etc. Buy a few things ahead of time at a garage sale so he has some toys he hasn't seen before.
• Make the car seat comfortable with soft padding.
• Decide beforehand that you are going to have fun.
• Make sure one adult on the trip is responsible for driving and the other for taking care of kids.
• Realize you may have fussy times but that they will pass.

(See also A-8, F-1.)

Thanks to Backyard Center Parents, Circle from Yakima, Washington

My son, fourteen months, won't keep his hands off the TV and stereo dials. What should I do?

- Take his hands off firmly and say, "TV is not to play with." Keep removing him gently.
- Be very consistent in not permitting him to play with the TV!
- Make a cover to put over the TV when not in use.
- Give him something else with lots of knobs to play with when he goes for the TV set.
- Try to find someone—like a grandpa—who will make a "knobby" box.
- Place the TV and stereo out of reach during this stage, so you can cut down on the "No's."
- Put masking tape over the knobs.
- We decided his exploring was more important than the TV show and let him do it until he got bored, which was soon after we stopped reacting.
- Buy a toy TV with knobs and have him play with that instead of the real one.
- Take the knobs off the TV. Use them only for on/off and volume.

Thanks to Backyard Center Parents, Circle from Yakima, Washington

What can I do about my baby's tantrums? She is twelve months old. She cries, hits me, and even bangs her head, and that scares me.

- Physicians say there is danger in head bumping. Get a helmet.
- Don't get angry yourself.
- Stay with your baby, hold her so she can't hit you, talk to her calmly, and let her know you love her even when she is angry.
- Think about changing your expectations of what you will get done during the day in case your baby is feeling too pushed.
- Put your baby into her crib and then leave her alone for a short time (two or three minutes).
- Don't give her attention for tantrums.
- Let your child know you are not afraid of her anger as you gently, but firmly, keep her from hitting you.
- Look at the before-tantrum times. See if there is something that seems to bring the tantrums on that you could adjust.
- Touch your baby, cuddle her, rock her lots when she is not having a tantrum.
- She seems young for this. Perhaps you could talk with a counselor about your scare.

(See also A-4, B-4.)

Thanks to Ellen Peterson, Circle from Lafayette, California

What can I do instead of hitting the baby when I'm exhausted?

- Get a sitter, get away, and give yourself a rest.
- Put the child in a safe place, go into the bathroom, close the door, and scream.
- Call a friend.
- Figure out some ways not to get so tired.
- Take a deep breath and count to ten.
- Hit a pillow.
- Read an old favorite letter or reread a list you had written earlier of ways in which you are a good parent.
- Get your feelings out so the child can see you are angry, but don't threaten or scare him.
- Go out and walk around the house (if the baby is in a safe place).
- Move away from your child and start whispering instead of yelling.
- Put the child in his crib for four or five minutes so you can have time out for yourself.
- This is the time to use the playpen.
- Put some calm, flowing music on the stereo and fix yourself a cup of tea.
- Learn and practice some meditation or relaxation exercises.

(See also E-9, H-3, H-5.)

Thanks to Carole Gesme, Circle from Minnetonka, Minnesota

At our house 4:00 to 7:30 P.M. is pandemonium time. How can I calm it down?

• Fix a casserole for dinner early in the morning or use a crockpot. Then you can play with the kids and not feel pulled about fixing dinner.
• Feed the children earlier sometimes.
• Listen to soft or danceable music during this time. Dance. Look at a book with the kids.
• Give the older kids jobs like setting the table to help get dinner ready.
• Go to the park for part of this time.
• See if an older neighbor child can come in to entertain your child (or children) for part of the time.
• Hire a sitter to come in every day from 4:00 to 5:00 P.M. You do whatever you need or want to for yourself.
• Feed the children some fruit at 4:00 P.M. and have some yourself.
• When your mom asks when she can help, ask her to come between 4:00 and 7:30 P.M. one day a week.
• Take turns with your spouse. One takes the kids for a walk while the other gets dinner ready.
• Keep frozen dinners in the freezer for days when the pandemonium is worse than usual.

Thanks to Pearl Noreen, Circle from Seattle, Washington

The fifteen-month-old daughter of a male friend of mine bites and hits me when I'm with her father. What shall I do?

- Learn the Being affirmations and say them to her, gently. (See page 11.)
- Remove her hand and say, "No, I can't let you hit me."
- Don't bite or hit her back. Show her how to be gentle.
- Plan an activity that you will both enjoy when you are with the child.
- Write or find affirmations for yourself and say them before you are with the child. (See page 11.)
- Ask her father to hold her firmly, but gently, and say, "No biting or hitting."
- Stop the biting now, but look for good qualities in the little girl.
- Get the biting and hitting stopped for everybody's sake. Sounds like this little one is distressed and may be threatened by her dad's caring for you. Give her time.
- Get down on the floor and play with her.

(See also E-4, E-7, H-9.)

Thanks to Sandra Sittko, Circle from St. Paul, Minnesota

I need options for physical exercises that I can do and still have my toddler with me.

- Set a routine for taking a brisk walk with your child in a backpack, riding a pedal or pushride toy, or being pulled in a wagon.
- Take advantage of the family and preschool swim programs at local recreation centers.
- "Mom and Me" exercise classes are offered through recreation programs.
- Try recorded disco or aerobic music in your own living room, and both of you dance.
- Look for folk dance groups that include children in classes.
- Invest in a child seat for your bicycle, and a child's helmet, and enjoy the bike trails in the area.
- Some roller rinks have child care available.
- Try jumping rope at home.
- If you like running, form a joggers' babysitting co-op and map out a route that goes past each member's home.
- If you can run at a park or school, take a babysitter along.
- Try a cross-country ski trip with the baby in a backpack.

Thanks to Gail Davenport, Circle from Seattle, Washington

What can I do when my child is screaming and the telephone is ringing?

- Choose not to answer the phone. Attend the child.
- Let it ring.
- If this is an ongoing problem, answer the call on an extension phone in another room and make the call short, really short!
- Ask another adult to take care of the child.
- Pick up the child, answer the phone, and ask if you can return the call later.
- Get an answering machine for your phone and call back later.
- This may be a time for a brief playpen interlude for your baby.

(See also H-8.)

Thanks to Backyard Center Parents, Circle from Yakima, Washington

I need options for arranging child care so we can get some time alone as a couple. Please include any ideas for overnight, evening, or daytime care.

- Ask relatives to babysit.
- Set it up with grandparents to keep the children at your house or theirs.
- See if you can trade child care with a neighbor.
- Set up a monthly babysitting exchange with another family that has children matching yours in age. You can use the time as a couple even if you choose to stay home.
- Make use of recreation facilities that offer child care, e.g., bowling and swimming pools.
- Set up a babysitting co-op that exchanges hours. Small co-ops can work just as well as larger twenty to fifty member co-ops. (See page 118.)
- Contact the Girl Scouts for referrals of teenage sitters who have had some training.
- Contact home economics teachers at the junior and senior high schools for referrals of reliable sitters.
- Connect with a licensed family day-care home that accepts part-time and drop-in children.
- Drop-in child care is available at some YWCAs and YMCAs. Check it out.

(See also I-8 and **How to Start a Backyard Center**.)

Thanks to Gail Davenport, Circle from Alderwood, Washington

F. Keeping Them Safe

How can I get my one-year-old daughter to get into, and stay in, the car seat without a big fuss?

- Use a firefighter's hat just for car time.
- Congratulations for starting at this early age! It becomes a habit and may save her life someday.
- Our car won't start until our child gets into the seat and is buckled in.
- Practice consistency. Don't deviate, not even once. Insist on using the car seat for *all* travel, not just in your car.
- Save special toys and books for your child to use while she is in her car seat only.
- Our child checks to see if I'm using my seat belt and vice versa.
- When you advance your daughter to a toddler seat, wrap it up and make it a special gift for her.
- As you buckle her up, play an imitation game where you do something like tapping your chin, and then she does the same.
- We say favorite nursery rhymes and sing songs as we buckle up in our car.
- Place a sticker on her car seat that she can look at or peel off.
- Recite, "I love you too much to let you out of your car seat. I want you safe," as long as necessary when the going gets rough.

(See also A-8, E-5.)

Thanks to Backyard Center Parents, Circle from Yakima, Washington

What can I do to keep my fourteen-month-old in the playpen?

- Arrange so he doesn't stay in it too long, like five to ten minutes.
- Give your child something safe and soft to have in the playpen with him.
- Play a special record he likes, if you have to put him in.
- Save the playpen for emergency/safety times only.
- My daughter never did stay in her playpen. She was too busy and her frustration wasn't worth it. Don't put any toys in that she could use to climb out.
- Put the playpen out where the rest of the family is. Use it only for safety, *not* convenience.
- Put the playpen next to the table where you're working.
- When you're exhausted and the baby doesn't object, putting him "in the pen" for ten minutes is a good idea . . . a rest period for you.

Thanks to Samara Kemp, Circle from Modesto, California

My daughter wants to stand up in the bathtub and I'm afraid she will fall. What can I do?

• Put a plastic laundry basket inside the tub. Allow her to stand in the basket while you hold on.
• Use a suction seat.
• Mount a bathtub hammock and let her hang onto that.
• Take a bath with her.
• Those molded, sponge baby tubs work really well.
• See if showering with her works.
• Use a firm grip and say, "Please sit down."
• Use a bathmat to cut down on slippage.
• When she stands, say "No" firmly and sit her down. If she stands again, take her out of the tub and end the bath.

Thanks to Backyard Center Parents, Circle from Yakima, Washington

My toddler gets into the silverware in the dishwasher. What should I do?

• Put plastic containers and other safe things into a drawer. Open that drawer for the toddler to play in while you do the dishes.

• It's a good thing that you are being careful. Children can break glass in the dishwasher.

• Place plastic plates and wooden spoons and forks in the dishwasher just for him. He can help by putting these in and taking them out.

• Keep spoons in the basket in the dishwasher for your toddler to play with. Then put forks and knives in later.

• Do the dishes when the child is occupied somewhere else. Corners of the dishwasher are sharp.

• If you let him play in the dishwasher, be sure to see that there is no detergent in it!

• I keep a stock of empty cans (coffee cans and such) for my son to stack in the dishwasher or bang on or roll on the floor. Be sure the cans have no sharp edges.

• Fill one bottom drawer in your kitchen with fun stuff for your toddler to empty out: clean dust cloths, empty grocery sacks, sponges, whatever. He'll love it!

• I wonder if they will enjoy doing dishes when we want them to?

Thanks to Melinda Scott, Circle from Walnut Creek, California

My sixteen-month-old screams and stiffens when I try to put her into the grocery cart, and she runs the other way when I let her out. She hurt herself by running smack into a gum machine because she was so intent on getting away that she didn't look where she was going.

- Leave your daughter at home with someone to care for her.
- Use a day care or neighbors for child care when you need to do grocery shopping.
- Let her ride on the bottom of the cart.
- Give her a job to do—carry bananas or hold the grocery list for you.
- See to it that you take a favorite toy.
- Keep in mind that this, too, will pass. This may be a way for your daughter to begin to establish her independence.
- Bring along a snack.
- Stop at the park on your way to the store. Tell your toddler this is her time to run.
- Avoid shopping trips at naptimes. Shop early in the day when you and she are both rested.
- Play a game, helping her identify familiar objects in the store. Let her choose a safe one to hold.

(See also E-7, F-1.)

Thanks to Nat Houtz, Circle from Edmonds, Washington

Grandma's house is not baby-proofed. How can I deal with this?

- Call your mother before you leave, to give her a chance to prepare.
- Pick up valuables and put them in a safe place when you first arrive.
- Ask Grandma to look for safe, interesting objects to put into a special drawer, like plastic spoons and containers, metal lids, and coffee cans.
- Ask Grandma to visit in your home and lovingly explain why.
- Make visits short and don't plan to stay overnight.
- Explain to her that your son can learn the difference between a crystal ashtray and a margarine tub later, after he has had plenty of chance to explore how things feel and stack.
- Affirm yourself for not wanting to say "no" all the time!
- Babyproof one room in Grandma's house. Get socket covers and safety locks. Use heavy rubber bands to lock cabinet doors. Bring them with you when you visit.
- Bring a special box of toys with you to keep your child busy.

Thanks to Backyard Center Parents, Circle from Yakima, Washington

Christmas is coming soon. We really want to have a tree, but how can I make it safe?

- Put your tree up on a table.
- Place your tree in the playpen.
- Don't decorate the tree. Just enjoy the fragrance of pine.
- Block off the tree so your child can't reach it, but be sure your child can still see the tree.
- Show your child how to touch, not grab the tree.
- Use a living tree, which will be in the house for a short time with no lights and unbreakable ornaments.
- Have a tree as you normally do, but keep the breakable ornaments near the top. You can use lights to teach the meaning of "hot."
- Tie the tree to the ceiling and floor. Place the valuable ornaments at the top. Put styrofoam balls and other safe ornaments at the bottom.
- Let your toddler have her own tiny tree with unbreakable ornaments that she can put on and take off the tree.

Thanks to Backyard Center Parents, Circle from Yakima, Washington

How can I safeguard my toddler from abduction?

• Never leave your child alone in the car.
• Discuss safety rules with your sitter about opening the door, going for walks, and answering the phone.
• Stay beside your child in public, always!
• Use a stroller strap or a backpack when you are shopping.
• Choose sitters with care. (See page 113.)
• Don't let your toddler wear a T-shirt with her name on it.
• Investigate your local police or Red Cross fingerprint program.
• Be consistent with your child in insisting that she stay with you.
• Trust your feelings about people who approach your child.
• Read *Jenny's New Game* by Laurella Cross, a book on how to prevent people from stealing your child. (See **Resources**.)

(See also F-9.)

Thanks to Backyard Center Parents, Circle from Yakima, Washington

I'm hearing so much about sexual abuse, and it worries me. How can I protect my child?

- It's up to you to be really careful about who he's around.
- Don't force him to kiss or hug relatives.
- It's the parents' job to carefully screen sitters.
- Tell your kids, "Nobody touches you there but Mommy and the doctor."
- Be aware of any changes in his genital area.
- When a child cringes from a neighbor, or doesn't want to go to someone's house or be near someone, *wonder why*.
- It's a good idea to teach your children that you have "surprises," *not* "secrets" in your family.
- Read him the book, *It's My Body* by Lory Freeman. (See **Resources**.)

(See also F-8 and **About Abuse**.)

Thanks to Educational Service District 105 Staff, Circle from Yakima, Washington

G. Who Raises the Kids

How can I handle grandparents who favor one of my kids over the others?

- Express your concerns by describing what they do and telling them what you want them to do.
- Say it as you see it, to *them*.
- Let them see only one kid at a time.
- Grandparents must be made aware of their behavior. Having the parents try to make it up to the neglected child doesn't work. The child knows full well what is happening.
- Point out that favoritism is a heavy burden for the favored child.
- You could stand up to the grandparents and tell them they can't come to your house without comparable presents for both children.
- Show the grandparents things they could do to favor all the children.
- I remind my parents often. They claim they are making up for *my* favoring one over the other. I wonder if they're right?
- Remind them that all children are born equal as far as needing grandparents is concerned. Ask how you can help them treat each one as a favorite.
- Tell them you know that they have enough love for all the grandchildren.

(See also H-10.)

Thanks to Backyard Center Parents, Circle from Yakima, Washington

How do we help grandparents not to feel rejected when our explorer doesn't want to be held and cuddled?

- If the grandparents and a parent sit together when the child is quiet, they all can get used to each other.
- Reassure them that parents can feel rejected, too.
- Say, "Mom, he's busy exploring now. He'll need loving later."
- Give each of them a chance to rock the baby to sleep and snuggle when he is sleeping.
- Give them the chance to bottlefeed or read a story to your toddler.
- Tell them that after this age of depending on Mom, there will come an age when he'll want to be with grandparents.
- Remind grandparents to explore with him by getting down on the floor and playing, stacking blocks and such.
- I suggest to my folks that they not immediately pick him up, but give him "warm up" time to get reacquainted.
- It's kind of you to care about your parents' feelings, but remember it's up to them *not* to feel hurt.
- Share Clarke's tape, *The Wonderful Busy Ones*, with them. (See **Resources**.)

Thanks to Backyard Center Grandparents, Circle from Yakima, Washington

My explorer loves to grab her grandpa's glasses. What shall we do to protect life and lens?

- Advise your father to take his glasses off when holding the baby.
- Insist that grabbing glasses is a no-no.
- Tell Grandpa to take the baby's finger and push it gently against the nose piece each time baby makes a grab. This really works!
- Buy a pair of toy glasses for your little one.
- Warn people with glasses that kids do make passes!
- This is a passing curiosity. In a few months glasses will be safe.
- Offer the child something else to play with while she is being held by a "glasses" person.
- Has Grandpa tried contact lenses?
- Be sure that all your grandfolks with lenses know about explorers and their curiosity. The toddlers aren't being purposefully naughty!
- Make a "poncho" for Grandpa to wear to distract your baby. Make one out of a terry cloth towel with a hole cut out of the center for the hands. Sew a variety of toys on.

Thanks to Backyard Center Parents, Circle from Yakima, Washington

The grandparents object to my picking up our six-month-old when he cries. They say he should cry it out. What can I do?

- Say, "I'd rather pick him up now than wait until his screaming reaches a desperate pitch, and teach him he has to be desperate to get my attention."
- You and your husband should present a united front, stating, "We decided to meet our baby's needs in this way and at this age."
- Say, "We want to build the baby's self-esteem by acknowledging him when he calls us."
- Crying is how a baby communicates.
- Tell them, "I am building my child's trust in me and the other adults who care for him."
- Turn the situation around and ask, "If you were crying, wouldn't you like me to comfort you?"
- Remind them that the family is the first place to teach your child that his needs are important. This teaches him to get his needs met later on.
- Remember that it is OK to stay with your values and beliefs, even when your parents disagree.
- See what they would think about reading the chapter on crying and spoiling in *The First Three Years of Life* by Burton White. He says you can't spoil a baby under eight months. (See **Resources.**)

(See also B-4, C-6, I-5.)

Thanks to Backyard Center Parents, Circle from Yakima, Washington

How should I handle the visiting grandparent who brings pop and candy for my explorer? We don't approve.

- Just ask your parents not to bring candy. Tell them that your child isn't allowed to eat candy.
- Get your child a T-shirt that says, "Please don't feed me candy."
- Say, "Please bring stickers instead of candy. The baby loves them."
- Ask them to bring fruit.
- Suggest that Grandma bake something special and healthful instead of bringing candy.
- Tell them hugs and kisses help kids grow better than sweets.
- Suggest some little picture books or inexpensive toys they could bring instead of candy.
- Have them bring fruit juice instead of pop.
- Limit sweets to one day a week. If grandparents come on that day, the kids can eat sweets.

Thanks to Yakima Valley Community College Cooperative Preschool, Eisenhower Parents, Circle from Yakima, Washington

My mom is pressuring me to toilet train my seventeen-month-old. He is not ready and neither am I. What can I do and say about this?

- Explain that most kids this age don't have enough awareness of how their bodies work to begin toilet training.
- Say, "It goes faster and easier when you train a child who is two-and-a-half or so because the sphincter muscles are ready then."
- Explain that you don't feel he is ready. Then, don't let yourself be pressured.
- Say, "Mom, I'm sorry, but we don't agree on this issue. Let's talk about something else."
- Find a way to remind Mom that it will be your decision and that you don't feel he is ready.
- Show her medical books that give reasons not to push an "unready" child or ask her to talk to your physician.
- Say, "Relax, Mom, I don't mind the diapers."
- Say, "I know you were expected to train us early. I'm so glad that rule has changed."
- Say, "No," and then don't do or say anything else.
- Assure her that there is lots of time and that he won't be carrying a diaper bag to school.

(See also C-6, G-4.)

Thanks to Yakima Valley Community College Cooperative Preschool, Central Lutheran Parents, Circle from Yakima, Washington

So many adults we know, and even some strangers, want to kiss our ten-month-old on the lips. What should I do to discourage this?

- Say, "It bothers me when you kiss my baby on the lips."
- Explain to the adult that your baby likes to be hugged.
- Make a game of touching other ways like an "Eskimo kiss."
- Be assertive and say, "Please kiss her on the cheek."
- Tell them you are trying to teach your child to turn her cheek.
- If all else fails, have your baby teethe on garlic buds!
- Show by example how to give and accept kisses on the cheek.
- Ask the person to play a small game or sing a song to the child instead.

Thanks to Backyard Center, Community-At-Large Grandparents, Circle from Yakima, Washington

My friend brings her explorer to play with mine and just lets her run wild. What should I do?

- Set down some simple rules at the beginning of the visit.
- Direct suggestions to the mother like, "Doris, I expect you to keep Jenny in this room. I have not childproofed the back rooms."
- Don't invite them back until the kids are in college.
- Establish a safe, "child-proofed" room and let the explorer loose.
- Try meeting your friend and her explorer someplace else besides your house, where you won't worry about your special things.
- Talk with your friend before she comes over and let her know your concern.
- This may be the time to make a "tent" with a blanket and chairs for the explorers.
- Gather together some safe toys that your explorers can play with in the same room with you.
- Get adults together in the evening, when the kids aren't around.
- If your friend won't take charge of her own explorer, it's up to you.

(See E-10, H-9.)

Thanks to Backyard Center Parents, Circle from Yakima, Washington

My husband didn't handle a situation with our toddler as I thought he should have. What can I do?

- Say, "This disturbs me. When can we talk about it?"
- Say, "Our kid is important. I think he needs a dad who does. . . ."
- Both of you have different opinions. If it's not harmful to the child, let the disagreement slide.
- Choose a calm time and tell your husband you are upset. Give him examples of what you would like him to do instead and why.
- Write him a note that says you don't have all the answers but that you want to talk about the incident and how you feel about it.
- Say, "It's your right to choose, and I want you to know my feelings about. . . ."
- Compliment your spouse when you like what he does.
- Read child development articles pertaining to your baby's stage of development and show the articles to your husband. Let him know you are still learning, too, or ask *him* to read the article or book and discuss it afterwards.
- I don't think it hurts kids to have parents disagree about little things. They'll sort it out.
- Take a parenting class together to help you decide on mutual goals.

(See also G-10, G-11, H-11.)

Thanks to Backyard Center Grandparents, Circle from Yakima, Washington

My ex-husband doesn't know very much about kids, but now he wants to have our daughter every weekend. What should I do?

- Ask him how he plans to take care of her and what he knows about the needs of explorers.
- What are his visitation rights? Do you think you need to challenge them? Call your lawyer.
- Send along your daughter's schedule and a list of food choices.
- Suggest that he take a parenting course to learn how to care for her.
- Ask him to take care of the baby for a couple of hours while you're away. This will help to break him in.
- Perhaps his mom could help out.
- It's OK for you to be concerned about your daughter's welfare. Find ways to see that she's protected. Call your local child protection service for ideas.
- Write a list of tips for making the weekend fun and safe. Include your child's favorite activities. Mention mannerisms that can aid him, for example, she pulls on her right ear lobe when she is tired.
- Be straight with your ex-husband. Let him know that you expect him to be responsible.

(See also G-9, G-11.)

Thanks to Gail Nordeman, Circle from Cincinnati, Ohio

Sometimes my wife does things with our kid that I don't like. What should I do?

• Ignore it, but let her know when she does something you do like.
• Tell her what a good mother she is and how much you love her. Then say, "I didn't like the way you did this because. . . ."
• Say, "I think it would have worked better if you had. . . ."
• I'd express my view, want to know what my wife's views were, then come up with a compromise on how to handle it next time.
• Tell her.
• Have a weekly meeting to discuss how to deal with the kids.
• Excuse yourself and your wife from the child quietly. Plan a united front and present it to the child that way.
• Be consistent with limits previously set up. If a situation arises that you didn't anticipate, play it by ear at that moment and decide later what the policy from then on will be.
• Tell your wife why you want her to do it another way.
• Read the *Father's Almanac* by S. Adams Sullivan. (See **Resources**.)

(See also G-9, G-10.)

Thanks to Backyard Center Parents, Circle from Yakima, Washington

H. Parents Have Needs and Problems, Too

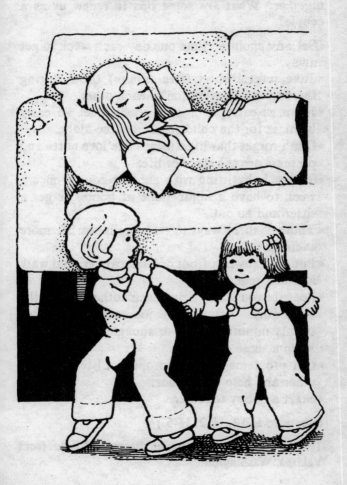

I thought a baby would make our marriage even better, but now we never seem to have any time together. What are some tips to renew us as a couple?

- Set an appointed time one day each week to get away.
- Take several short (five-minute) times during the day to pay attention to each other.
- From as early an age as possible set an early bedtime for the child so you can be alone.
- Don't forget that little things like love notes and presents are the spice of life.
- Switch babysitting with another couple once a week to have a night alone at home, or get a sitter and go out.
- Think of three ways to make your sex life more exciting.
- Put the baby in a front or back carrier, and walk and talk together.
- See if you can help each other with the housework. After each job, take fifteen or twenty minutes to talk or snuggle.
- Keep a sense of humor.
- Get problems out in the open. Listen to each other and help each other.
- Start a hobby together.

(See also E-13, H-2, H-5.)

Thanks to Backyard Center Parents, Circle from Yakima, Washington

I'm so tired I don't feel like having sex. What can I do about this?

- Have a babysitter come in one hour per day, or even once or twice a week. Do *whatever* you want to do—clean a closet, read a magazine, rest.
- Tell your husband how tired you are and ask him to help solve this problem.
- Tell your husband that you really love him and that you are too tired to have sex tonight. Consider having sex sometimes in the mornings.
- See if your husband can come home during the baby's naptime if you have more energy then.
- Hire help for housework.
- Nap with your child.
- Every two weeks, at least, go out with your husband. Be consistent about doing this.
- Have a regular, early bedtime for your baby so you can have more time with your spouse.
- Be sure you are getting enough vitamins for extra energy.
- Have your hemoglobin level checked.
- Agree with your husband on which days you will skip the housework and keep that energy for loving.
- Are you nursing? Many women are not as interested in sex while they are nursing.

(See also H-4.)

Thanks to Nat Houtz, Circle from Seattle, Washington

I feel like I'm all "boxed in." I no longer do the things I used to do for fun. How can I find time for myself?

- Put your baby in front of a mirror, or in a swing, and have a good supply of reading material close by to "take you away" for ten minutes or so.
- Do fun things during your baby's naptime. The cobwebs can wait.
- Join a babysitting co-op, or ask Grandma to watch your child.
- Plan and schedule a once-a-week appointment with a sitter so that you will be sure to go out and it won't be an option.
- Get your baby into the routine of an early bedtime.
- Get up earlier while your baby is still sleeping.
- On weekends take turns with your spouse taking care of the baby. Read Sandy Jones' *Crying Baby, Sleepless Nights*. (See **Resources**.)
- Ask your librarian for a time-management book or article that will help you find shortcuts.
- Unplug the phone.
- Make a list of priorities and put yourself near the top. Remember, it is okay to take care of yourself.

(See also E-3.)

Thanks to Judy Popp, Circle from Yakima, Washington

I'm pregnant with my second child. With my explorer still waking up at night and my having to run after him in the daytime, how can I get more rest?

- Be sure to nap when your explorer naps. Let housework wait.
- Alternate with your husband in getting up at night.
- Take "mini-breaks" for five to ten minutes. Put your feet up, play soothing music, and/or read.
- Give yourself permission to ask a friend to watch your explorer when you need help.
- Encourage Dad to take the explorer for a twenty-minute walk or a ride every day. Relax while they are gone.
- On weekends take turns with your husband sleeping in.
- On your spouse's night to get up with the explorer, sleep in another part of the house so you'll sleep through the night.
- Exchange babysitting with a friend who also needs more rest. You take the 1:00 to 2:30 P.M. shift while she rests. You rest from 2:30 to 4:00 P.M. while she watches the kids.
- Save the playpen for times when you are physically exhausted. Put baby in it and curl up nearby for a few minutes without sleeping.

(See also B-2, H-2.)

Thanks to Backyard Center Parents, Circle from Yakima, Washington

How can I get enough rest? I have two kids under two years.

- As soon as both children go down for a nap, leave the housework and go to bed yourself.
- Let housework slide a little. Reevaluate your priorities.
- Take advantage of any help. You are worth it!
- Swap sitting with a friend so you have one afternoon a week to yourself.
- Get help. Make lists of resources and use them.
- Keep meals simple. Use convenience foods.
- Use disposable diapers or a diaper service.
- Remember, you don't need to be perfect to be a good parent.
- Have Grandma take the kids once a week while you sleep.
- Get a sitter to come in for one hour every day after school. Lie down or listen to a relaxing tape.

(See also B-2, E-13, H-2, H-4.)

Thanks to Backyard Center Parents, Circle from Yakima, Washington

As a single parent, I spend all my time with my little girl. How can I find some other grown-ups to be with?

- Join Parents Without Partners, or a child care co-op, (see page 118) or start a Backyard Center group (see page 114).
- Take your little girl to visit some nursing home folks. Often they are hungry to see children and will talk with both of you.
- Call a Tupperware lady and ask to be invited to a party.
- Join a church where there's an adult Sunday School class for you and a nursery for your little girl.
- Look in the Sunday supplement for classes that offer babysitting or "Mom's Day Out" ads.
- A co-ed sports activity, like volleyball, might be a lot of fun!
- You could trade babysitting with a friend so you have the time to get out and do these things.
- Sell Shaklee, Amway, Avon, or one of those products, and go to the meetings.
- Take a class at the community college. And don't be in a hurry to leave the minute the class is over.
- Go to story hour at the library. Other parents will be there, too.

(See also E-11.)

Thanks to Backyard Center Parents, Circle from Yakima, Washington

I feel guilty that my seventeen-month-old doesn't mind me better. How can I handle this?

• Remove as many items as you can that you don't want her to get into. Then you don't have to say "no" as often.

• Tell your baby that she's doing a good job of exploring the world. That's her job right now, and she'll be at the "minding" stage soon.

• Read the chapter about six- to eighteen-month-olds in Clarke's book, *Self-Esteem: A Family Affair*. (See **Resources**.)

• Buy a doll or teddy bear for yourself—one that will "mind you."

• Find ways to spend less time with the people who help you feel guilty.

• It sounds as if you're feeling guilty about spending so much time feeling guilty! Could you be expecting too much of both you and your explorer?

• Check out some other seventeen-month-old children and relax a bit.

• Remember that at seventeen months your child will still need you to provide a safe environment.

• Join a support group for parents of toddlers.

(See also H-8 and **Ages and Stages**.)

Thanks to Backyard Center Parents, Circle from Yakima, Washington

Whenever I'm on the telephone my toddler gets into everything. How can I talk on the phone without feeling so frustrated?

• Pick up your child while you talk on the phone.
• Sit on the floor with him while you're talking.
• Get a play phone and have him use it at the same time.
• Limit your phone calls to five minutes.
• Put a collection of toys into a basket that the child is not allowed to play with unless you are on the phone.
• Hold your toddler in your lap and let him play with something special.
• Ask the caller if you may call back during naptime.
• If the call is an emergency, put the child into the crib.
• Expect him to play near you and give you a few minutes of time. Have chalk and a chalkboard near the phone.
• Put your child in a high chair and talk on the phone while he uses crayons and paper.

(See also E-12, H-7.)

Thanks to Backyard Center Parents, Circle from Yakima, Washington

What are ideas for correcting another child in my home when her parents are not acting on the problem?

- State the problem without piling on any judgment. "If I see your child getting into something unsafe or inappropriate to play with, I'll go ahead and take care of it."
- Say, "In our family we don't play with the TV dials, but you can turn the dials on this busy box." Find something the child can do instead when she does something inappropriate.
- Give a house tour to the parent, pointing out areas that are off-limits and those in which the children can play.
- Make sure there are toys, boxes, blocks, and other interesting and safe things to play with.
- Invite the parents over without the kids, or just don't have the family over until the children are older.
- Move yourselves into the child-proofed area so you can watch the kids.
- Avoid the problem by visiting with your guest on the couch. Pull the couch away from the wall far enough so that the child can play behind it in her own special spot. Give her some interesting and safe toys or kitchen gadgets.
- Put a sheet over a card table so the child will have a hideaway.

(See also E-10, G-8.)

Thanks to Backyard Center Parents, Circle from Yakima, Washington

My brother's baby and mine were born six days apart. Now they are already being compared at seven months. What can I do to discourage this?

- Give your brother Brazelton's *Infants and Mothers* to show him the range of *normal* development. (See **Resources**.)
- Redirect the conversation. Don't talk about your baby's achievements.
- Tell them you are not into competition. Then don't get caught up yourself by comparing.
- Children deserve the right to grow without being compared.
- Ask your brother and his wife to practice enjoying each child as if he were the only one.
- Tell the adults to compete with other adults instead of setting up competition between babies.
- Stress differences in "normal" children. Each body grows at its own rate. By the time children are eighteen years old, nobody will care who was first, unless you make a big deal of it.
- Be "tactfully blunt" and ask the person to stop comparing.
- Try to befriend your nephew despite the competitive atmosphere.
- Tell a story of when you were compared as a child and how you didn't like it.

(See also A-1, G-1.)

Thanks to Backyard Center Parents, Circle from Yakima, Washington

How can I get my husband to spend more time with our baby?

• Tell him the baby deserves to know her dad. Tell him babies react with dads in ways they don't react with moms, and your baby deserves both experiences.

• Reinforce the positive interaction your husband already has with the baby.

• It is not your responsibility. It is *his* responsibility.

• If you want Dad to interact with the baby, show Dad what he's doing right, not just what he's doing wrong.

• Let the father be alone with the child.

• Children take one-half of their rearing from each parent. Ask him if he wants his half to be blank.

• Buy a copy of S. Adams Sullivan's *Father's Almanac*. (See **Resources**.)

• Tell him you wish he would hold the baby more often.

• If he doesn't know how to be with a baby, tell him to go ahead and practice.

(See also G-9, G-11, I-4.)

Thanks to Backyard Center Parents, Circle from Yakima, Washington

The doctor just told me my baby is handicapped and said that she may need to be institutionalized. I feel terrible.

- I'm sorry.
- Get a second opinion.
- Share your grief with someone.
- Join a support group. Your doctor can probably tell you about one.
- Do whatever you need to do to learn not to blame yourself.
- Get support and information from at least one other parent whose child has the same handicap.
- Write "Dear Abby" and find out if there is a national support group for parents with a child like yours.
- Check and see if your area has a Parent-to-Parent Program that will match you with a family that has a similarly handicapped child and has been through it. Call your local public health department.
- Get some counseling. Talk about how you feel as many times as you need to.

Thanks to Backyard Center Parents, Circle from Yakima, Washington

How do I know whether to bring my sick baby to our church nursery or friend's home?

- Check with your physician *first* to see what the child has and if it is contagious.
- Don't bring your child if she is running a temperature.
- Don't bring your child if her nose is running.
- Don't bring your child if she has a visible rash.
- If you must bring your child, keep her and her things separate and at a distance from other children. Realize that it takes only one toy from a sick child to spread infection.
- Leave your baby with a sitter.
- Ask if there are any guidelines for bringing ill children to your play group or nursery.
- Establish guidelines with your friends as to when and where not to bring sick children when you are visiting one another.
- You probably wouldn't want your child to be exposed unnecessarily to illness. Show the same courtesy to others.

Thanks to Backyard Center Parents, Circle from Yakima, Washington

I. Working Parents

How can I get everything done and get to work on time?

- Shower the night before. Have your clothes and baby's clothes all laid out.
- Get your spouse to share the transportation-to-sitter duty.
- Pack the diaper bag at night with an extra set of clothes.
- Ask your babysitter if your baby can arrive with his sleeper still on and have breakfast at her house.
- Find a quality sitter who will come to your house in the mornings.
- Ask your boss if you can start your work a half hour later and stay later.
- Think about the things that absolutely have to be done. For instance, try leaving your bed unmade.
- Try making your own breakfast simple, like a liquid protein drink.
- Supply your sitter with an extra set of clothes, food items, disposable diapers, etc., so that you're only packing supplies once or twice a week.
- Share morning duties with your spouse, so that one person isn't burdened with all the "nitty-gritty" of getting out of the house.
- Forgive yourself for what doesn't get done, and go to work peacefully.

Thanks to Backyard Center Parents, Circle from Yakima, Washington

How can I have more time with my baby when I work full-time?

- Keep dinners simple. Stock up on high protein snacks and buy frozen entrees.
- Eat out occasionally. Use paper plates when you don't.
- Visit baby during your lunch hour.
- Use a diaper service in your area.
- Hire a high school student or a cleaning service to clean house once a week.
- Fold diapers as you need them and use disposable diapers.
- For dirty dishes: Fill sink in the morning to soak. Wash once a day or buy a dishwasher.
- Ask other working moms how they cut corners.
- Start a movement at your office for an employees' day-care center right there!
- Remember that verse about "The cobwebs can wait!"
- Read *2001 Hints for Working Mothers* by Gloria Mayer. (See **Resources**.)

Thanks to Backyard Center Parents, Circle from Yakima, Washington

What can I do about our daughter crying every day when I leave her at the sitter's?

- Remember, this can be a normal phase at this age. Don't feel guilty.
- Leave something of yours (glove, hankie) with her to keep until you come back.
- Always let your child see you leave. Don't sneak away to avoid her crying.
- Prepare a "surprise bag" with different things for her to play with each day.
- If it happens all the time, try another sitter or make arrangements for one to come to your house.
- Have your husband take her to the sitter. Maybe that will make a difference.
- Help your child start with an enjoyable activity before you leave.
- Give your daughter a chance to be upset. You stay calm.
- Establish a good-bye ritual, like a kiss on each cheek and your saying, "I love you and I'll be back after work."
- Affirm your child's feelings. Say, "I'm sorry you're sad about my going, but I need to go! See you soon, special kid."

(See also A-9, I-1, I-8, and **About Abuse**.)

Thanks to Yakima Valley Community College Preschool Cooperative Parents, Circle from Yakima, Washington

How can I get my husband to share more of the household responsibilities?

• Find some ways to share with him the ideas in Letty Pogrebin's book *Family Politics*. (See **Resources**.)

• Sit down and explain your needs. Get your feelings out.

• Ask for help. Make a list of things that you need help with.

• Have your husband take full care of the baby and do house chores for a day. It's called making him aware.

• Together list all the chores that need to be done on squares of paper. Put the slips of paper in a basket and have each partner draw one until they're all gone. Do the ones you draw!

• Working on the jobs together takes less time. Then you can plan an outing or just plain "cuddle."

• At our house my husband usually does the outdoor chores, like mowing the lawn, hauling wood, and fixing the car. Sometimes we trade chores or work together.

• Say, "I need help! Should I quit work, get a cleaning person, or will you agree to divide the chores?"

(See also G-9, G-11, H-11.)

Thanks to Backyard Center Parents, Circle from Yakima, Washington

My mother thinks I should stay home with the baby, and I want to pursue my career.

- Find good care for your child with a person who shares your values and then reassure your mother.
- Point out some benefits your working has for your family.
- Remember that wanting to pursue your career doesn't mean you love your child less.
- If you need the income, tell your mom that. Expect her to trust your decision to work.
- Invite your mom to help with child care as much as she'd like, if you are willing for her to do that.
- Trust your own feelings about wanting to pursue your career.
- Hug your mom. Let her know you appreciate her concern, but that you need to follow your own decision.
- Perhaps your mom needs reassurance that you feel she was a good mother even though she didn't have a career.
- This can be a good time for both of you to realize that you can disagree about something important and still love and value each other.
- Consider her reasons. Consider yours. Consider the baby's welfare. Then decide.

(See also C-6, G-4, I-6.)

Thanks to Melanie Weiss, Circle from Bellevue, Washington

My husband is pressuring me to go to work, and I want to stay home.

- Stay home if you can. They are little only once!
- Find a part-time job that you will enjoy!
- Find a job you can do at home like telephone sales, typing, ironing, or sewing.
- Start your own day-care center.
- Read and share with your husband Burton White's *First Three Years of Life*, page 247, where he encourages moms to stay home for the first three years.
- Rank your family's needs. Perhaps you can give up material things to stay home.
- Set time-limited goals such as work for a year to save money; then quit.
- Borrow money now; pay back when child is older.
- Collect data about Moms working from books like Selma Fraiberg's *The Magic Years*. (See **Resources**.)
- Plan a time when the two of you can sit down and really talk about what you want—quality of life as well as quantity of material things.
- This is a time when a counselor, or perhaps your minister, can help you both sort out your goals. If your husband won't go, you can still see a counselor yourself.

(See also I-5.)

Thanks to Backyard Center Parents, Circle from Yakima, Washington

How do I deal with my guilt about going back to work?

• If you can, cut down your work hours. If you can't, leave your job at work and make the most of at-home time.
• Go home for lunch.
• Work when your spouse can watch the child.
• Find the very best child care you can.
• Join a working parents' support group.
• Celebrate your child's milestones—first steps, waving bye-bye, first word—instead of feeling guilty about things missed.
• Remember that past generations seldom were able to be full-time parents. So enjoy your provider role and your mothering one, too.
• Allow yourself twenty minutes a day to feel really guilty. Then spend the rest of the time knowing you're a very energetic and interesting person, who's a better parent because you work.
• Have a special, sacred time each day that you spend with your child. Don't allow interruptions, not even phone calls!
• Use some of those hard-earned bucks for a cleaning person. It's worth it, and you'll have more time to spend with your child—guilt free!

(See also I-6.)

Thanks to Backyard Center Parents, Circle from Yakima, Washington

What do I look for in a quality day-care provider?

- Find someone who enjoys and values time with children. Look for someone who has some activities planned for each day.
- Find someone who is comfortable with you and will tell you things as they are.
- Look for clues at the end of the day, like a play area that is neither too disarrayed nor super neat.
- Drop in unexpectedly to get a "feel" for things. Watch how discipline, crises, and routines are handled.
- Look at the ages and numbers of kids being cared for. One adult is needed for every two or three explorers.
- Look for someone whose feelings on discipline and child care are similar to yours.
- Ask for recommendations from friends. Then go with what feels right to you, trusting your "gut."
- Choose a provider who *does* use car seats but *can't* stand playpens (as a regular thing).
- Look for a provider who is licensed by the state and can offer references. Also set up your own standards for safety, hygiene, routines, and learning ideas.
- See how your child feels about this place and person, and how he reacts to going back there.

(See **How to Set Up a Child-Care Co-op.**)

Thanks to Backyard Center Parents, Circle from Yakima, Washington

How to Start a Backyard Center

A "Backyard Center" is a program that provides parent education and support for families of newborns to five-year-olds. There are two types of Backyard Centers: "Parent-Infant Support Groups" (birth to two-year-olds) and "Homestyle Preschool Play Groups" (two- to five-year-olds).

"Parent-Infant Support Groups" of six to eight families meet in each other's homes on a rotating basis. Parents bring their infants (birth to twenty-four months) and the host or hostess acts as a discussion leader on a selected parenting topic, leads Suggestion Circles, and leads baby songs and infant stimulation exercises for the infants.

In the "Homestyle Preschool Play Groups" the parents rotate being play group hosts for the two- to five-year-old children from all the families. One helper parent assists the host, and the rest of the parents have the time off. After the children have played in each home, the parents and children meet for a "cycle" meeting, using the same meeting format as the "Parent-Infant Support Groups."

Any interested parents can begin their own Backyard Center group. The key to the success of the group will be the commitment of the members. The goals of the group are decided by the members. The meetings should be fun, flexible, and something to look forward to.

How to Start Your Own Backyard Center Parent-Infant Support Group

Recruit Members. Make use of hospital birth records, YWCA and YMCA preschool programs, physicians, Lamaze classes, co-op babysitting groups, community bulletin boards, and local newspaper ads, etc.

Organize. When four or more families have expressed interest, meet with them and

1. Decide on the day of the week, time of the day, length of the meeting, and how frequently to meet (most popular times are weekly or biweekly for one or two hours).

2. Discuss a rotation system in which each family takes a turn as the host/discussion leader of the group.

3. Exchange addresses and phone numbers and any other pertinent information.

4. Plan your calendar for the month.

Design the Format. Each meeting can be divided into four parts: (1) a parenting topic, (2) Suggestion Circles, (3) baby songs and exercises, and (4) a snack.

1. *Parenting Topic.* Host/Parent selects from the following:

• Present a topic or article from a magazine, book, or newspaper to the group. (Example: "Sleep Disturbance," "When to Wean Your Baby," etc.)

• Share information on community activities, workshops, and programs offered that are appropriate for parents of infants so that other members of the group are aware of what's going on in your community.

- Organize a craft project (making a mobile or homemade toy.)
- Arrange to attend a class or workshop together.
- Arrange for a speaker to present such topics as nutrition (how to make your own baby food, for example), appropriate and safe toys, stimulating language, self-esteem (your own and your child's), reading to infants, and how and when to discipline.

2. *Suggestion Circle*. Lead parent asks who wants a Suggestion Circle. Follow the guidelines in this book. (See page 122.)

3. *Baby Songs and Exercises*. Babies love to be sung to, and singing can calm down a whole troop of crying babies. Adapt any song you know to a baby exercise. It's fun and babies don't mind if you sing off-key! Parents can practice doing infant stimulation using infant exercises or massage books. (See **Resources**.)

4. *Snack Time*. Optional, but it is an excellent time for conversation and sharing of concerns.

You can organize a "Backyard Center Homestyle Preschool Play Group" in the same way, except that the parents' meetings are held only after the children have played in each home. You can organize your Backyard Center program on your own, or you can persuade a school district, YMCA, YWCA, or other community agency to sponsor it.

The "Backyard Center" Program originated in 1975, in the Yakima school district in Yakima,

Washington, and is designed to provide cost-effective parent education and support to families of newborns to five-year-olds. The district offers help in recruiting and organizing of the groups, provides facilitator/presenters for the individual group "cycle" meeting every six to eight weeks, and develops parent-child activity packets. In addition, the district staff provides occasional workshops on parenting topics where all the Backyard Center groups get together at one time.

—Judith L. Popp

How to Set Up a Child-Care Co-op

1. Start small. Four to ten families allow several possible exchanges without many complications.

2. So you can begin with trust, start out with people you know and whose child-rearing ideas are similar to yours. Sponsor new members.

3. Visit each other's homes with your children before you leave your child for care. The environment should feel familiar and safe to parents and child.

4. Decide whether your co-op will be limited to babies and preschoolers or will also include school-age children. Remember that homes are best equipped for the ages of the children who live there.

5. Set some geographic boundaries for your co-op.

6. Discuss whether your co-op will be used for daytime, evening, weekends, or overnight care.

7. Establish a health policy. Include guidelines for sick children, and provide a medical release form to be signed by parents and left for each child being cared for.

8. Recommend that members carry liability insurance.

9. Select a secretary and rotate the job.

10. Develop a system for recording hours. The secretary can keep an index card listing the

care given (+ hours) and care received (− hours) for each family. Total the cards each month and pass them on to the next secretary.

11. Decide if you want to arrange care through the secretary only, or between members. If you arrange time between yourselves, report hours only to the secretary.

12. When more than one child from a family is left for care, decide how to credit each member. Two children could total either two times or one and one-half times the total hours.

13. The member arranging for care should leave emergency information with the caregiver (including destination, car license, and phone number).

14. Members must agree on whether the caregiver will be allowed to run errands with the children in the car.

15. Insist on using car safety seats, and leave your child's seat with the caregiver.

16. If a meal will be served to your child, decide whether the caregiver will receive an extra half-hour credit.

17. Provide each member with a membership list, rules, guidelines, and emergency forms. If you can't get someone to donate duplicating costs, spread the cost among the members.

—Gail Davenport

Where to Go for Additional Support

If you have talked with your family and friends, tried the ideas in the Suggestion Circles, read some child-rearing books, and still feel stuck with a problem, here are some places to call for additional help or to find out about parenting classes. If you have difficulty finding a telephone number after looking in both the white and the yellow pages, call any of these sources and ask them to help you find the number you need.

Community Services

Crisis or hot-line numbers
YMCA, YWCA, or a local church or synagogue
Chemical abuse prevention programs
Chemical abuse treatment centers
Community civic centers
Women's or men's support groups
Battered women's and children's shelters
Local hospitals
Alcoholics Anonymous
Parents Anonymous

Private Services

Psychologists, social workers, psychiatrists, therapists, family counselors

Schools

Community education (local school district)
Colleges or universities

Community colleges
Vocational and technical schools

Government

Community mental health services
Public health nurse or department
Child protection services
Family service agencies
County social service agencies

Interview the persons who will help you to see if they know about the area in which you need help. If you don't get what you need, go somewhere else until you do.

—The Editors

How to Lead a Suggestion Circle

The Suggestion Circle is a technique for collecting ideas. It is the opposite of brainstorming. Use it to activate clear thinking and tap the wisdom of the group.

As the leader, do the following:
1. Ask people to sit in a circle.
2. Contract with the person who has the problem to be a listener and to accept each suggestion with no comment other than "thank you."
3. Ask that person to state one problem in a clear, concise way.
4. Ask someone else to make a written list of the suggestions so the listener can give full attention to listening.
5. Ask the people in the Suggestion Circle to center their bodies, think carefully for a moment about possible solutions to the problem, and to each give one high-quality, one-or-two sentence "You could..." or "I would..." suggestion. They are to go in order around the Circle and are not to comment on or evaluate each other's suggestions.
6. When the suggestions have been given, remind the listener to take the list home and decide which suggestion to use.

A Suggestion Circle of twelve persons takes from three to five minutes to complete.

—Jean Illsley Clarke

Conclusion

Many times the most encouraging and helpful support to parents of explorers comes *not* from child-care experts and other professionals but from veteran parents who have already been through this stage of parenting. The old saying "two heads are better than one" describes the merits of this book for coping with typical concerns and problems that crop up during the explorer stage, from six to eighteen months.

As we researched and collected Suggestion Circles from over fifty parent support groups, we learned the following:

- Parents are not alone with these concerns. The problems are typical and common for most families.
- Parents dream great dreams and want the best for their children and themselves.
- Parents are good thinkers and can help one another.
- There can be more than one solution to a problem.
- Parenting is a constant growing process as we read, listen, and experience. Parents aren't born with the innate knowledge of what is best to do.
- Parenthood can bring about conflicting feelings of confusion, uncertainty, and isolation. Lack of confidence is common in new parents. On the flip side, parenting can also bring feelings of euphoria and great joy, as we watch our children unfold and become

We trust that you will use this book to fit you and your explorer's needs. Know that you are a caring and capable parent. Give yourself permission to take time out from your "ONEderful" toddler to rest and play a little yourself. Take a new class, buy a new shirt, meet a friend for lunch, or go to the library and soak up the silence! *You deserve it!*

—Judith-Anne Salts

Resources

Badger, Earladeen. *Infant/Toddler: Introducing Your Child to the Joy of Learning.* Englewood Cliffs, N.J.: Instructo/McGraw-Hill, Inc., 1981.

Bernath, Maja. *Parent's Book for Your Baby's First Three Years.* New York: Ballantine Books, 1983.

Brazelton, T. Berry, M.D. *Toddlers and Parents.* New York: Dell Publishing Co., 1974.

_____. *On Becoming a Family.* New York: Dell Publishing Co., 1981.

_____. *Infants and Mothers.* New York: Dell Publishing Co., 1983.

Brown, Saul L., M.D. *Infant and Toddler Sleep Disruptions* (Audiotape). Los Angeles: Preschool and Infant Parenting Service, 1983.

Burck, Frances Well. *Baby Sense: A Practical and Supportive Guide to Baby Care.* New York: St. Martin's Press, 1979.

Burtt, Kent, and Kalkstein, Karen. *Smart Toys for Babies from Birth to Two.* New York: Harper Colophon Books, 1981.

Caplan, Frank. *The First Twelve Months of Life.* New York: St. Martin's Press, 1978.

Cass-Beggs, Barbara. *Your Baby Needs Music.* New York: St. Martin's Press, 1978.

Church, Joseph. *Understanding Your Child from Birth to Three.* New York: Pocket Books, 1973.

Clarke, Jean Illsley. *Self-Esteem: A Family Affair*. Minneapolis: Winston Press, Inc., 1978.

_____. *The Important Infants* (Audiotape). Minneapolis: Daisy Tapes, 16535 Ninth Avenue North, 55447, 1983.

_____. *The Wonderful Busy Ones* (Audiotape). Minneapolis: Daisy Tapes, 16535 Ninth Avenue North, 55447, 1983.

Cross, Laurella Brough. *Jenny's New Game*. Englewood, Colo.: P.O. Box 4025, 80155, 1983.

Diagram Group. *Child's Body: A Parent's Manual*. New York: Paddington Press, Ltd., 1977.

Eden, Alvin N., M.D. *Positive Parenting*. New York: New American Library, Inc., 1980.

Fienup-Riordan, Ann. *Shape Up with Baby*. Seattle: Pennypress, 1980.

Fraiberg, Selma. *The Magic Years*. New York: Doubleday & Co., 1980.

Freeman, Lory. *It's My Body*. Seattle: Parenting Press, 1983.

Gonzalez-Mena, Janet, and Eyer, Dianne Widmeyer. *Infancy and Caregiving*. Palo Alto, Calif.: Mayfield Publishing Co., 1980.

Gordon, Ira J. *Baby Learning Through Baby Play*. New York: St. Martin Press, 1970.

Hagstrom, Julie, and Morrill, Joan. *Games Babies Play* and *More Games Babies Play*. New York: Pocket Books, 1979.

Johnson & Johnson. *First Wondrous Year*. New York: Macmillan Publishing Co., Inc., 1976.

Johnston, Lynn. *Hi Mom, Hi Dad! The First 12 Months of Parenthood (101 Cartoons).* Deephaven, Minn.: Meadowbrook Press, 1977.

Jones, Sandy. *Crying Baby, Sleepless Nights.* New York: Warner Book, 1983.

Kantner, Carol N. *And Baby Makes Three.* Minneapolis: Winston Press, Inc., 1983.

Kelly, Marguerite, and Parsons, Elia. *The Mother's Almanac.* New York: Doubleday & Co., 1975.

Kelly, Paula, M.D. *First Year Baby Care.* Deephaven, Minn.: Meadowbrook Press, 1983.

Kunhardt, Dorothy. *Pat the Bunny.* New York: Golden Press, 1942.

Lansky, Vicki. *Practical Parenting Tips.* Deephaven, Minn.: Meadowbrook Press, 1980.

Leach, Penelope. *Babyhood.* New York: Alfred A. Knopf, Inc., 1974.

————. *Your Baby & Child: From Birth to Age Five.* New York: Alfred A. Knopf, Inc., 1974.

Levin, Pamela. *Becoming the Way We Are.* Wenatchee, Wash.: Directed Media, Inc., 1974.

Levy, Dr. Janine. *The Baby Exercise Book.* New York: Random House, 1973.

Marzollo, Jean. *Supertot.* New York: Harper Colophon Books, 1979.

Mayer, Gloria Gilbert. *2001 Hints for Working Mothers.* New York: Quill, 1983.

Mayle, Peter. *Baby Taming.* New York: Crown Publishers, Inc., 1978.

Montagu, Ashley. *Touching: The Human Significance of the Skin*. New York: Harper & Row, 1971.

Pogrebin, Letty C. *Family Politics: Love and Power on an Intimate Frontier*. New York: McGraw, 1983.

Richards, Martin. *Infancy: World of the Newborn*. New York: Harper & Row, 1980.

Rozdilsky, Mary Lou, and Banet, Barbara. *What Now? A Handbook for New Parents*. New York: Charles Scribner & Sons, 1972.

Schneider, Vemala. *Infant Massage: A Handbook for Loving Parents*. Toronto: Bantam Books, 1979.

Segal, Marilyn. *From Birth to One Year*. Rolling Hills Estates, Calif.: B. L. Winch & Associates, 1974.

Segal, Marilyn, and Adcock, Don. *From One to Two Years*. Rolling Hills Estates, Calif.: B. L. Winch & Associates, 1976.

Sullivan, S. Adams. *The Father's Almanac*. New York: Doubleday & Co., 1980.

Thevenin, Tine. *The Family Bed: An Age Old Concept in Childrearing*. New York: Dantree Press, 1977.

Warren, Jean. *More Piggyback Songs*. Everett, Wash.: Warren Publishing House, 1984.

White, Burton L. *The First Three Years of Life*. New York: Avon Books, 1975.

————. *A Parent's Guide to the First Three Years*. Englewood Cliffs, N.J.: Prentice-Hall, Inc., 1980.

Williams, Sarah. *Round and Round the Garden*. New York: Oxford University Press, 1983.

About the Editors

Jean Illsley Clarke, M.A., is the author of the book *Self-Esteem: A Family Affair* and of the parenting program of the same name. The Suggestion Circle technique comes from that program. She is a Transactional Analyst, a parent educator, is married, and a mother of three. She watches children in the exploratory stages to relearn how to explore her own environment.

Darlene Montz, M.Ed., writes a weekly newspaper column and tapes public service announcements for parents on radio. She coordinates preschool special education programs for Central Washington school districts, supervises an alternative high school's nursery project, and advocates for families in transition. Married and the mother of three, Darlene has a granddaughter, Lauren, who obligingly explored her way through the six- to eighteen-month stage during the creation of this book.

Judy Popp, M.A., has three adult children who went through their explorer stage while she was completing both bachelor's and master's degrees in education. Currently the Director of Early Childhood programs for Yakima, Washington's school district, Judy created its Home-School Partnership, and now supervises its Home Base project. Judy has been active in parent education efforts for twenty years, having spearheaded many school-community networks. Judy gets multi- generational learning about exploring from her mother, Marjorie, husband, Harry, and grandchildren, Casie Elizabeth and Travis.

Judith-Anne Salts, B.A., coordinator of Yakima School District's Backyard Center program and designer of its Parent-Infant support groups, is a resource to several hundred young families. Her advice is sought about nutrition and night lights, sitters and separation. Formerly a first-grade teacher, Judi derives practical expertise from her life with daughter Robin, twelve, and son Christopher, fifteen. Her husband, Dennis, is exploring "what the next book will be about."

Index

132

Other Learning Materials Available

Developmental Tapes, by Jean Illsley Clarke. These audio cassette tapes present important information about children and the nurturing they need. Told in entertaining and easy-to-understand language from the perspective of children of different ages, the tapes describe child care by parents and by day-care providers. The stories allow adults to set aside fear or guilt and have the distance they may need to hear the information presented. The tapes, told in both male and female voices, are also useful tools for helping older children understand their little brother's and sister's needs and behavior. Each story is twelve-to-eighteen minutes long; at least eight spaced listenings are recommended.

Ups and Downs with Feelings, by Carole Gesme. This collection of games features a game board with a wide variety of "feeling faces" to help children and adults identify feelings and learn ways to be responsible for them. Included are directions for seven separate games, one of which uses the affirmations printed in this book.

Affirmation Cards. Tiny colored cards, with a separate affirmation printed on each, that can be read, carried, or given as gifts.

For more information, including prices, write to

Daisy Press
16535 Ninth Avenue North
Plymouth, MN 55447